beginner's guide to
long distance
running

beginner's guide to
long distance
running

SEAN FISHPOOL

Published in the UK in 2004
exclusively for
WHSmith
Greenbridge Road
Swindon SN3 3LD
www.WHSmith.co.uk
by Tangent Publications, an imprint of
Axis Publishing Limited.

Conceived and created by
Axis Publishing Limited
8c Accommodation Road
London NW11 8ED
www.axispublishing.co.uk

Creative Director: Siân Keogh
Designer: Sean Keogh
Project Editor: Michael Spilling
Production Manager: Toby Reynolds
Production Controller: Jo Ryan
Photographer: Simon Punter

Text and images copyright
© Axis Publishing Limited 2004

Note
The opinions and advice expressed in
this book are intended as a guide only.
The publishers and author accept no
responsibility for any injury or loss
sustained as a result of using this book.

ISBN 1-904707-07-6

9 8 7 6 5 4 3 2 1

Printed and bound in China

contents

beginner's guide to long distance **running**

introduction

Taking up running should be an offer you cannot refuse. For the cost of a pair of running shoes you gain membership in a health club that is open 24 hours a day, and is never more than a few minutes away. More importantly, it is a free passport to a side of yourself you may never have enjoyed before—a healthier, more relaxed, more confident you. And running will take you to that new you faster than any other activity.

the benefits of running

The best thing about running is that it can be exactly what you want it to be. There are no rules: you can run by yourself, with one friend or with 10; you can run just to clear your head and unwind at the end of the day; or you can follow a schedule to achieve distances and times you never thought possible. When you run, you are joining more than 15 percent of the population of the United States and

here's what running can do for you

weight loss Running burns calories faster than any other activity. One mile of running uses 100 calories; just a 30-minute run can burn 250–500 calories.	**quiet time** Forget about your to-do list for 40 minutes— simply breathe fresh air and enjoy being alone with (or without) your thoughts.
better health Running boosts your body's immunity to illness. Run for 145 minutes a week, for example, and you will be 40 percent less likely to suffer a heart attack. It improves your blood cholesterol level, and it fights diabetes, arthritis, and osteoporosis.	**more energy and a better body** Exercising will help your body work more efficiently, with improved metabolism and cell regeneration. Your body's lean-to-fat ratio will improve, and your calves, thighs, hips, and buttocks will become stronger and shapelier.
less stress Runners are less prone to depression than sedentary people. This is partly because of the endorphins that the body releases but also because they enjoy the benefits of achieving something.	**healthier lifestyle** Running will make you think about your lifestyle. You will very probably adopt better sleeping habits and give up smoking and heavy drinking. Many runners also prefer to eat healthier foods.
confidence You will feel better because you know that you are fit and motivated and achieving your running goals. This will inspire you in other areas of life.	**a knowledge of your body** You will discover what kinds of effort your body responds to best. If you race or do speedwork, you will find out how your body reacts to pressure.

Europe who already enjoy the health-boosting, fat-burning, stress-busting benefits of regular exercise.

This book is designed to help you, whatever your ability and your reasons for taking up running. There are day-by-day training schedules for beginners and experts alike, and you will find simple running advice that will guide you in everything from buying your first shoes to selecting foods for eating during a run.

One of the best things about running (along with its fitness benefits) is that it is a cheap sport—you only need a pair of good running shoes, shorts, and a T-shirt to begin.

SUCCESS STORY: sarah yates

Journalist, 34 Sarah has always been a gym goer, but she never quite found the fitness she was looking for. She was doubtful when a gym instructor suggested that she spend more time on the treadmill, but she began a schedule and stuck to it. She had soon entered a local 5K (three-mile) race, and fired up by the camaraderie there, she set her sights on a 10K race two months later. Now she's a regular. She runs her local trails three times a week, and tries to run a race once every two months.

SUCCESS STORY: simon jordan

Advertising Director, 47 Simon took up running because he was 30 lbs overweight. He had to take things gently at first, slimming down and building up his fitness with two months of brisk walking and swimming. By the time he began to incorporate a series of two-minute jogs into his walks, he was surprised by how natural they felt. Over three more months he extended the jog intervals until he found that he could keep jogging for 30 minutes without a break. By this time he had already lost 20 lbs. A year later he is happily running four or five times a week.

getting started

After reading the last few pages, you are probably halfway out the door already. But—if you can hold on for just a little longer—you can equip yourself with all the information you need to build lasting foundations. This introduction answers your basic questions, ensures that you are ready to start running safely, and shows you how to use this book to become a full-fledged runner in just a short time.

how to use this book

The first chapter covers shoes, clothing, and accessories; eating and drinking; stretching and keeping your body strong; and all-important motivation. These pages will be useful to all levels of runners. They are designed to be dipped into—you do not have to sit

Developing into an effective runner is within everyone's grasp, regardless of their age.

down and digest all the information before you go for your first run.

Later in the book you will find six training levels (remember to first read the safety checks on pages 9–11). Some runners will start at the first level and work their way through to whichever level their body and their determination takes them. Others will want to meet a specific need—say an upcoming 10K race.

There are schedules for everyone: Level 1 is for beginners, while Level 6 will train experienced runners to complete a marathon in less than three hours or a 10K race in 35 minutes. Each level contains schedules for racing and for fitness, so they are ideal whether you have a precise goal or you simply want to head out of the door without

1 starter level

Complete beginners. Four days a week of running and walking.

2 starter level

Relatively new runners who can run 30 minutes nonstop, three to four days a week.

3 refresher level

Lapsed runners and those who can run 15–30 miles (25–50 km) over four or five days a week.

4 intermediate level

Regular runners who can run 25–35 miles (40–55 km) over four to six days a week.

5 upper level

Experienced runners training five to six days a week, including those who want to run a 3:30–4:15 marathon.

6 upper level

Experienced runners training six to seven days a week, including those who want to run a 2:45–3:30 marathon.

I don't have the time

You only need 20–30 minutes, three to four times a week, to benefit from running—no other activity is so efficient. You will be surprised at how easily you can fit it in, especially with the support of your partner or family.

Am I too fat?

No—there is a runner in all of us, whatever our shape! If you are more than 20 percent over your ideal weight, however, you should ease into running via a combination of regular brisk walking and nonweight-bearing exercise such as cycling or swimming (see pages 38–39).

I have weak knees or ankles

Running can strengthen your joints and muscles. To help your joints, choose shoes that give you adequate support and cushioning (see pages 16–17), and run on soft surfaces where possible (see "The Five Best Running Surfaces," pages 10–11.)

Am I too old?

It is never too late to benefit from running, unless you have a medical condition that prevents you. Recreational runners in their 60s regularly embarrass younger competitors at races of all distances. Running will help to strengthen your bones, and reduce the risk of heart attack—but do check with your doctor before you begin if you are over 40.

Am I too slow?

Absolutely not—and if you need proof, just go along to a local race and witness the wonderful variety of runners who take part. Whether it takes you five minutes or fifteen minutes to complete a mile, you are a runner as long as you keep putting one foot in front of the other.

I have a medical condition

It is true that running simply may not be suitable for a few people, and may require special caution from others. See the safety advice on page 11, and consult your doctor if you have any doubts.

having to think about what to do that day. You could run simply by following your instincts, but it is easier and safer—and much more effective—to follow some kind of program. Even an extremely simple schedule will pay dividends. Why? Because it will build up your fitness as fast as possible while giving your body the rest days and easy days it needs to get stronger and to avoid injury.

A program will help you to avoid the common pitfall of trying to do too much, too soon, which often leads to burnout; and it will lead you steadily to your goals (see pages 40–41 to find out why goals are so important).

first steps

Every runner has to begin somewhere. If you want to set off on the right foot, adhere to the following principles, and you are not likely to go wrong.

Good quality running shoes are a must for anyone who wants to run in comfort and avoid serious injury.

set a goal

Whether it is a short race, a long race, a weight-loss target, or simply the aim of being able to run 30 minutes nonstop, give yourself a specific goal, write it

down, and pin it up where you will see it often. Make the goal attainable but significant to you, and set a time frame for achieving it. This is a guaranteed way to stay motivated (see pages 40–41 for advice on setting targets).

proper running shoes

Buy proper running shoes—this is the only purchase you really need to make, and it need not be expensive. It will minimize injury risk and help to make your first running steps a comfortable experience. Try to go to a running specialty store, to make sure your individual needs are assessed properly. Proper running clothes will make you feel (and look!) better, but they are not essential (see pages 14–23 for more about shoes, clothing, and equipment).

the five best running surfaces

smooth trail
Dirt, woodchip, or forest trails are naturally cushioned—they are also likely to lead you through beautiful and inspirational surroundings. For safety, always run with a partner.

short grass
This is another soft, forgiving surface. It is best to avoid longer grass in case hidden holes or ruts lurk beneath the surface.

running track
Maybe not exciting, but flat and cushioned running tracks will also measure an exact quarter-mile per lap, so you can gauge your pace and record your progress from week to week.

find a running companion

Consider persuading a friend to take up running with you—or find out about joining the beginner section of your local running club. The support and motivation will be invaluable.

heart-rate monitor

A straightforward monitor costs less than a pair of shoes, and can be a real help in making sure you run at a pace that is right for you. (See page 22 for more about choosing a monitor, and page 48 for simple, effective advice about training with one.)

go!

Don't wait any longer. If you have passed the safety check and you have purchased proper running shoes, turn to the first day of your schedule, and make some progress today!

SAFETY FIRST

- Do you have a heart condition?
- Does your family have a history of heart disease?
- Have you ever been told that you should only do physical exercise recommended by a doctor?
- Do you feel chest pain when physically active?
- Have you ever had chest pains when not active?
- Do you ever lose balance due to dizziness?
- Do you have a bone or joint problem?
- Are you taking drugs for blood pressure?

If you answered "yes" to any of these questions, consult a doctor before doing strenuous exercise.

- Also, take special care to progress your running carefully and listen to your body if you are more than 40 years old, or if you have not exercised regularly over the last five years.

AVOID

asphalt
Not the softest surface, but not the hardest either—and it is smooth. Ideally, run no more than two-thirds of your mileage on asphalt, and always wear good shoes to avoid injury.

treadmill
Cushioned, flat and safe, treadmills are convenient, even though they lack the inspiration of running outside. The action of running on a moving belt can slightly unbalance your running muscles, so integrate strength training and road running where possible. Treadmill running is great for those coming back from injury.

concrete
Essentially this is crushed rock, and it is the most jarring surface your body can encounter.

curved surfaces
Roads are curved at the edges, to allow drainage. If the curve is severe, it can damage your body over time. Avoid sharp curves if possible, and at the very minimum, change direction as often as possible.

1

the right stuff

To become an effective runner, you need all the support you can get. This section provides that support by arming you with all the information you need on eating the right food (both in training and for race days), avoiding injury, cross-training for greater fitness, and wearing the best clothing and footwear to help you be a comfortable, contented runner. Most important of all, you can also learn how to set goals and motivate yourself for many years of happy, effective running.

sole mates

Finding the right pair of running shoes can take some time, but it always pays off. Pick a pair just for their price or their looks and the chances are that you will leave yourself open to problems. Arm yourself with the following advice and head to a specialist retailer, however, and you will not go far wrong.

make fit a priority

You will not run far in badly fitting shoes. For most runners, a broad forefoot (to allow room for your toes) and a narrow rearfoot (to keep your heel and ankle snugly in place) make a good combination in a shoe. Remember that you will need roughly a thumb's width between your big toe and the end of the shoe to keep blisters at bay—many people find they need running shoes that are a size larger than their normal shoe size. It is very useful to know the basics before you buy a running shoe.

a shoe for your needs

A good all-around shoe combines cushioning (to lessen the impact on your joints and tissues) and stability (to keep your body aligned correctly). The amount of stability you need depends on your gait—that is, the movement of your foot as it goes through the cycle of hitting the ground and pushing off from the toes (see page 95). If your feet roll inward too much ("overpronate"), you need added stability to restrict this. If your feet do not roll inward as much as they should ("underpronate," or "supinate"), you need plenty of cushioning to encourage movement. If

a few tips on finding the right shoe

COST
Cost is not an indication of quality. There are some good shoes at low prices, especially if you have no stability problems or you are a low-mileage runner.

STYLE
Do not buy general sports shoes. Specialist running shoes are designed to meet the demands of running and are a must if you want to be comfortable.

TEST
Test the shoes before buying them to make sure they are right for you. Some stores provide a treadmill or allow you to jog around (or if dry, outside) the shop.

WEIGHT
A light shoe may seem ideal, but it can be a fast route to injury, as it may not provide the cushioning and stability you need for everyday training.

your feet are normal (or "neutral"), you can choose a shoe that lies somewhere in between. A knowledgeable store assistant or a biomechanics expert can help to analyse your gait (see pages 16–17, "Natural Selection," for more information about this).

When looking for shoes, you will come across a lot of technical names (such as Asics Gel or Nike Air). Many of these refer to the various patented cushioning and stability devices inserted into the shoes' foam midsoles, but do not worry too much about the subtle differences— the overall construction and feel of the shoe is far more important. If in doubt, do not panic—go to a specialist running store for professional advice. If the staff cannot explain pronation and shoe construction, go somewhere else where they can.

how long should my shoes last?
The length of a shoe's life depends on the runner, the type of shoe, and the running surface. The challenge for the runner is that you cannot always see when a shoe is worn out and needs replacing. Usually the midsole is the first part to break down (that is the thick foam layer between the removable insole and the hard rubber outsole). This reduces the shoe's cushioning and stability, which exposes you to the risk of injury. Try to keep a record of your mileage, and be sensitive to unexplained aches or pains. You can also look for clues such as a distinct tilt to the shoe when you place it on a flat surface; and a brittle or very creased midsole.

Some runners prematurely wear out the uppers or outsoles of a shoe, but usually these areas are not reliable indicators of its life span. Generally, the heavier you are, and the lighter or softer the shoe, the faster it will lose its cushioning and stability. Finally, the softer the surface you run on (grass, for example, is excellent), the longer both the midsole and the outsole will last. Runners and shoes vary so much that it is impossible to generalize about shoe life spans, but on average you can expect around 400 miles of good performance from a shoe. A heavy runner might only get 250–300 miles; a light, efficient runner might get more than 600 miles from one pair of shoes.

These running shoes contain gel in the forefoot and heel to provide extra cushioning.

natural selection

Running shoes fall into three main categories, which reflect three different types of biomechanics. There are also three further categories for specialized types of running. Ideally, it is best to have your biomechanics analyzed by a specialist practitioner or running shoe expert—if you cannot, a standard stability shoe is a good starting point. Remember that although cost is not a guarantee of quality, you do tend to get what you pay for—but your priority should be to find a shoe that is well-fitting and appropriate for your needs.

looking after your shoes

To maximize the life of your shoes, keep them in cool, dry conditions and wash them by hand; never put them in a washing machine with detergent or tumble-dry them, as these methods will damage them. When they do get wet, dry them at room temperature.

◀◀ cushioned

Straightforward shoes for runners with no biomechanical problems, or for people with inflexible feet. Often the lightest and softest category. Note that all running shoes are cushioned, not just this particular kind.

performance shoes ▶▶

These are fast-paced shoes with less cushioning and support than everyday shoes. Used by lighter, quicker runners for brisk training, or by normal runners for racing and speedwork. They usually weigh between 10–11.5 oz (280–320 g) for a U.S. size 9 (UK 8).

◀◀ motion control

These are heavy-duty shoes for runners whose feet don't roll inward enough ("underpronate"), and for heavier runners who need maximum support.

racing ▶▶

These are minimalist shoes with very low weight and maximum responsiveness. They are designed for light, efficient runners, and some are only suitable for short distances. They typically weigh between 7.5–9 oz (200–260 g).

◀◀ stability

Shoes with some added stability features, for runners whose feet tend to roll inward a little too much ("overpronate"). For many, they provide an ideal blend of smoothness and support.

off–road "trail" ▶▶

"Trail" shoes have added grip for soft or muddy conditions. Only a few types work really well. Studded fell-running shoes are a more extreme version. They are light, with limited cushioning and support but extraordinary traction.

staying cool

You can run in an old cotton T-shirt and shorts, as long as they are loose-fitting—but specialized running clothes are more comfortable, and may make you feel inclined to run more frequently. Choose synthetic fibers—they are lighter and warmer than cotton when wet, and many are specially designed to move sweat away from the skin so they feel drier.

basic summer clothing

In the summer, you will need light, cool clothing that does not restrict you. Most runners find that a T-shirt and shorts are enough. Items made from synthetic fibres, such as polyester, are better, since they won't make you sweat as much as heavier cotton clothing.

sports bra

In both summer and winter this is a must for women (regardless of bust size). Normal bras reduce breast movement by around 35 percent, but a good sports bra achieves closer to 60 percent. A- and B-cup sizes normally suit crop-top styles; larger sizes require molded cups. Either way you should look for a bra designed for high-impact activities.

running shorts

Normal running shorts have a light outer layer (usually with a side split for freedom of movement) and a built-in brief. You may want to wear lycra cycling shorts under your running shorts if your legs are prone to chafing. Either option should be light, dry, and comfortable.

running tights

On cool summer evenings, you might prefer to wear a lightweight pair of full-length running tights or pants. These are usually made from lycra and are very comfortable.

technical socks

These use wicking fibers to keep your feet dry. Look for a snug fit, and consider a wool and nylon mix for wet conditions, as it stays warm and comfortable when damp.

wicking vest

In the warmer summer months, many runners prefer to wear a sleeveless wicking vest. Wicking vests move sweat away from the skin to the outer surface of the fabric, where it evaporates.

wicking T-shirt

Like wicking vests, wicking T-shirts feel light, cool, and comfortable against the skin, and are a good alternative to cotton, which feels heavy and damp when you sweat.

beating the elements

Despite the cold and rain, winter running can be a truly unique and pleasurable experience (no really!). Just remember three guidelines (see opposite page) and you will enjoy running in the winter as much as in the summer.

basic winter clothing

For winter running, your clothing needs to be lightweight but protective. A lightweight running jacket, running pants and a long-sleeved thermal top are essential. A vest is less restrictive and very useful in milder weather.

lightweight running jacket
Runners produce a lot of sweat, so a lightweight, breathable jacket that lets perspiration escape is a comfortable option. A jacket that breathes well will not only be showerproof, but it will also be wind-resistant, which helps to stave off a chill. Most runners avoid fully waterproof jackets because they cause the body to become hot and sweaty. Technical fabrics such as Klimate keep water out but breathe so sweat evaporates.

light, long-sleeved thermal top
Also known as a "base layer," this is a synthetic, long-sleeved T-shirt woven to trap warm air within it. You wear a base layer next to your skin, either by itself on mild days, or under another layer in poor weather. For comfort, a close fit is best.

running tights or pants
A pair of close-fitting running tights, or slightly looser running pants with ankle stirrups, are lighter and faster-drying than cotton sweat pants. Tights tend to be warmest, especially when wet.

vest

These light, sleeveless jackets have legions of running fans. They keep the core of your body warm, while leaving your arms unrestricted and your torso well ventilated. They are normally windproof and showerproof.

waterproof suit

Some runners like the protection of a lightweight, fully waterproof jacket, even if it can cause them to sweat a little. Waterproof overpants can also be used in cold and stormy conditions.

running comfort

AVOID COTTON It gets wet and stays wet. That makes you uncomfortable, and more importantly, draws valuable heat from your skin. Instead, choose synthetic fibers such as polyester. These stay warmer when they are wet because they do not absorb moisture, and they are often designed to transport moisture from the skin to the outside of the fabric where it can be evaporated. (For more information on wicking T-shirts, see page 19.)

DON'T OVERDRESS Discovering the right balance between being too cold and overheating is a fine art, but plan to be a little chilly when you leave the house—after a few minutes' running you will soon heat up. If you are warm as soon as you start, you will be sure to overheat at some point during your run.

USE THE LAYERING PRINCIPLE This means wearing two or more thin layers in preference to one thick one, which gives you the versatility of being able to add or remove a layer as your body temperature changes. Most runners do not need more than two layers, and often find a long-sleeved wicking top and a lightweight jacket to be a successful combination. Zip-necks help with ventilation, too.

reflective gear

On dark nights, you need to be clearly visible to traffic. You can buy a lightweight, reflective vest cheaply; also, many shoes, jackets and pants carry reflective patterns.

runner's helpers

There are many different items that can help you with your runs, especially if you are preparing for a race. Watch lap timers are useful for monitoring progress run-by-run and week-by-week, while many runners use heart-rate monitors, which can be used to gauge whether to speed up or slow down depending on the kind of run. Other items, such as a thermal hat and gloves, are valuable, depending on weather conditions. Apart from the on-the-run equipment featured on these pages, many runners like to keep a training log to record their progress. Training logs can be very useful if you are preparing for a race, as they can record the key ingredients and stages in any previous preparations and monitor developments as they occur.

◀◀ heart-rate monitor

This will help you gauge your speed for a particular session. Products range from heart-rate only monitors to models that calculate your training zones, count calories burned, and store your heart-rate readings for you to consult afterward.

watch with lap timer ▶▶

A digital watch that can record your lap times is useful for marking your progress and helping you to understand pace. In races, it can tell you whether you are on target as you pass each mile marker. Most running watches come with anything from 8- to 300-lap memories.

◀◀ waist pack

These should be stable and fit snugly around the waist. They can be used to carry gels, candy, and other equipment. Some have water bottle attachments.

headwear ▶▶

The easiest way to lose heat on a winter run is through the head, so a thermal hat can make a big difference. Also, if you run in the summer sunshine, a lightweight peaked cap is useful to protect your head from harmful rays.

◀◀ water bottle

If you are training for more than 30 minutes, you should increase your fluid levels as you run (see page 27). Carriers include bike-style water bottles carried on a bottle belt, and hand-held bottles—though be careful that the larger ones don't unbalance your running style.

gloves ▶▶

Lightweight, thermal gloves can make a tremendous difference to your winter running, as much body heat is lost through the hands. They can also be removed during a run for easy temperature regulation. Many are made in reflective colors.

diet—food groups

Eating is a pleasure, and we want to keep it that way. With a few basic guiding principles, your diet can provide you with all the necessary fuel and building blocks for an active, rewarding lifestyle. You will run well, look great, and you certainly won't need to go through hell to get there. In the following pages you will learn how to construct a balanced diet to eat and drink effectively around a run. Take a look at these five main food groups.

food groups

carbohydrate

Carbohydrate is essentially energy food. There are two main types of carbohydrate—simple (sugars) and complex (mostly starches)—and you need a balance of both to be healthy. The glycemic index (see page 95) of a food—not just whether it contains simple or complex carbohydrates—determines the speed at which energy is released into the body. Foods with a high glycemic index (which give a rapid rise in blood sugar) include bread and potatoes, as well as bananas, raisins, and sugars such as glucose. Moderate glycemic index foods include pasta, noodles, oats, oranges, and sponge cakes; and low glycemic index foods include apples, figs, plums, beans, dairy products, and fructose.

fruit and vegetables

Fresh fruit and vegetables are nutritional powerhouses. If you eat at least five portions a day you will meet the body's quota for vitamins A and C, and gain potassium, fiber, and carbohydrate. Dark-green, leafy vegetables include plenty of iron, which benefits the blood. Broccoli, spinach, peppers, tomatoes, and carrots are particularly good options.

protein

Protein helps your body to build and maintain muscles, tendons, and fibers. The most obvious sources are meat and fish (which also contain the highest number of essential amino acids). Vegetable proteins are important too, and peas, beans, nuts, lentils, and seeds can provide your daily requirement. You need two servings of protein a day.

weight control ▸▸

If you want a guaranteed weight-loss plan, try this: exercise more and eat more healthfully. This is easier said than done, but nearly everyone who takes up running loses weight. Also, eating healthy food does not mean eating less—it just means eating thoughtfully.

fats

Fat is essential for proper cellular functioning, for the protection of internal organs, and for carrying the fat-soluble vitamins A, D, E, and K. Most of us eat more than enough fat, but if you severely restrict your intake, you risk harming your body.

milk and dairy products

Dairy foods help to keep your bones strong, because they are high in calcium, and they also contain protein and riboflavin, which is used in metabolism. All runners need calcium, but especially women under 20 or above 50, who should aim for four servings a day. One serving equates to a small carton of low-fat yogurt, three slices of cheese, or a small glass of milk. Canned fish and broccoli also contain calcium.

take a realistic look at what you eat

One way to avoid bad eating habits is to plan your day's eating in advance. Take healthy snacks such as bagels and dried fruit to work in order to avoid the vending machine.

make small changes

Change your diet gradually—turn to low-fat milk instead of whole milk, and replace one or two red-meat meals a week with vegetarian alternatives.

eat little and often

Healthy snacking (or "grazing") throughout the day burns more calories and keeps your body better fueled than eating big meals.

run more

Every mile you run uses around 100 calories, no matter at what speed. Build up slowly, and if you are already running at your safe limit, consider adding another activity to your routine.

run harder

Increasing the intensity of your runs burns more calories. Once you have become a regular runner, incorporate speedwork, hillwork, or threshold runs into your routine.

Remember that the calorie-deficit principle works best in moderation. Burning 500 calories a day more than you use, for example, gives you a safe and maintainable weight loss of about one pound a week. If you approach or exceed a deficit of 1,000 calories a day, your body will fire up defense mechanisms designed to retain as much weight as possible. You will also spend a lot of time being hungry, and you will become lethargic and probably irritable.

refueling around a run

eating

When you run, your body takes its energy from easily accessible muscle glycogen (stored, processed carbohydrate), and less accessible fat reserves. We all have fat reserves, but we need to ensure that our glycogen levels are high before, during, and after our runs. That is where smart eating comes in.

before a run

Some people can run within 30 minutes of snacking; others have to forego food for hours to exercise comfortably. Pre-run eating isn't essential on runs of less than an hour, but long outings take a little planning. A little readily available energy makes a difference—a bagel and a glass of fruit juice works well for most people. Remember to avoid too much fat and protein, as they are hard to digest.

during a run

It can be worth refueling with energy on runs longer than 45 minutes, and between repetitions in short, intense speedwork sessions. Keeping your stomach comfortable is essential, so avoid solid foods, except perhaps easy-to-digest favorites such as sports bars and jelly beans. Consider using sports drinks or gels (see page 31).

after a run

Eating 30–60 minutes after a run will help to minimize stiffness and soreness, especially after a hard effort. Research has shown that the best recipe for muscle recovery is fluid, plus a carbohydrate meal incorporating slightly less than 30 percent protein. You can buy special recovery drinks and bars, although a bowl of cereal with low-fat milk and a banana is a good homemade alternative.

drinking

Runners do not drink enough. The body needs water for almost all of its functions, including energy release and temperature control—and yet when we under-drink we wonder why we find training and racing really hard work. Even on inactive days, you should try to drink at least eight glasses of water. You need more when you run. In hot conditions, your body can lose almost four pints through sweat in an hour, which is enough to significantly impair performance.

before a run

You should be well hydrated before you run. This does not mean grabbing a cup of water just beforehand; rather, you should sip little and often throughout the day, and especially the afternoon and evening before a long morning run or a race. Aim to drink a pint of water (roughly half a liter) half an hour before you train.

during a run

You won't normally need to drink on runs of less than an hour, but on hot days it can be positively dangerous not to rehydrate more regularly. When you drink, sip little and often rather than gulping. On long runs, a safe rule is to take one small cup of liquid for every 15–20 minutes of running.

after a run

In order to restore its fluid balance, your body needs to take in twice as much water as you lose through sweat. Get into the habit of drinking more than normal for at least two or three hours after you run, and stick to water or a sports drinks containing sodium and low levels of carbohydrate. Weighing yourself before and after a run will show precisely the amount of liquid you have lost: 1lb equals 1pt (1kg equals 1l). You will know when you are properly hydrated because your urine will be pale.

balancing your diet

A runner's body needs a combination of carbohydrate, protein, and fat to keep it energized and healthy. Read the chart below for the correct balance and examples of ideal foodstuffs. Remember that the percentages relate to calories, not weight. This is very important, because one ounce of fat contains more than twice the calories of one ounce of carbohydrate or protein. It is simple, really—burn more calories than you eat, and you will lose weight.

low fat versus low calorie

So why do we worry about whether the calories in our diet come from carbohydrate or fat? Partly because of

Why can't we be more specific about the number of ounces of carbohydrate, protein, and fat the body needs each day? Because your daily calorie requirement depends on many factors, including your metabolism, your exercise levels and your gender, as well as your weight (see "Your Calorie Needs," far right).

YOU NEED	SO EAT THE FOLLOWING:
carbohydrate	
60–70 percent Approximately 0.1 oz per lb of body weight per day (4–6 g per kg).	Pasta, rice, potatoes, oats, bananas, raisins, figs, plums
protein	
15 percent Approximately 0.03 oz per lb of body weight per day (1.0–1.5 g per kg).	Meat, fish or seafood, dairy products, nuts, peas, beans and lentils
fat	
15–25 percent (40 percent monounsaturated, 40 percent polyunsaturated, 20 percent saturated) Approximately 0.02 oz per lb of body weight per day (0.4–1.1 g per kg).	Fats, oils, butter, peanuts, avocados and dairy products, such as whole milk and yogurt

During longer races, experts suggest runners should eat around two ounces of carbohydrate for each hour of running.

YOUR CALORIE NEEDS

You can calculate your approximate daily calorie needs like this:

1 basal metabolic rate

These are the number of calories your body uses at rest.

MEN:
11 calories per lb of body weight (24 calories per kg)

WOMEN:
10 calories per lb of body weight (22 calories per kg)

2 lifestyle

Add 30–40 percent for a sedentary occupation.
Add 50–60 percent for an active occupation.

3 exercise

Add 100 calories for every mile you run.

For example, a man weighing 150 lb (68 kg) would have a basal metabolic rate of approximately:

1,650 calories (11 x 150)

He would add 30 percent for a very sedentary occupation (495 calories), and 500 calories for five daily miles. That gives him a daily calorie need of roughly:

2,645 calories

These figures are only guidelines—your basal metabolic rate and even the efficiency with which your body extracts calories from food are very individual factors.

the harmful cholesterol associated with many fats; but also because it takes almost no effort to convert excess dietary fat into body fat.

By contrast, 25 percent of the calories in excess carbohydrates are burned in the conversion process. Sadly, this doesn't mean that a "low-fat" label is a green light for a pig-out—the other 75 percent of any excess carbohydrate calories still have to be stored.

eating for a marathon

Eating properly is the final flourish to careful marathon preparation. Here is all you need to know:

the days before the race

Runners used to deliberately starve themselves of carbohydrate in the week leading up to a marathon, and then gorge themselves in the last few days in the hope of filling their muscle glycogen stores to the maximum. However, now sports scientists recommend eating a balanced diet of up to 70 percent carbohydrate in the final week. You don't need to eat more than usual: as your training eases off in the last few days, you will automatically store a surplus of energy.

the night before the marathon

Eat a high-carbohydrate, low-fat, moderate-protein meal—pasta with a tomato sauce is a classic and effective option. Do not eat to the point of discomfort—between 800 and 1000 calories is plenty. Drink well, especially through the penultimate day.

the morning of the race

Drink 1 pint (500 ml) of water as soon as you get up, then sip water throughout the day of the race. Eat breakfast, even if it means getting up especially early to allow for digestion. Eat a low-fat option that you have

remember

Dehydration due to fluid loss is one of the prime causes of runners hitting the "wall" during a marathon—so keep taking fluids even when you don't feel thirsty.

GREAT DAYTIME SNACKS

dried apricots
fresh fruit
salted, unbuttered popcorn
fig rolls
chocolate bar (but just one...)
pretzels

eaten before in longer training runs—muesli, oat cereal, toast, and bagels are all ideal pre-race foods.

during the race
You should aim to replace 600 calories on the run to stave off sudden exhaustion and hitting what runners call the "wall." Energy drinks and gels are ideal (see below). It is also critical that you drink regularly to avoid dehydration and exhaustion.

after the race
Restock your body's energy supplies as soon as possible if you want to recover quickly and with the minimum of soreness (see pages 26–27 for advice).

SUGGESTED MARATHON-WEEK MEALS

breakfast
Bagel with honey
Orange juice or fruit smoothie
A little cereal with low-fat milk

Porridge (oatmeal) with raisins and honey
Orange juice or fruit smoothie

lunch
Baked potato with spiced baked beans and a little grated cheese
Fresh fruit salad

Chicken, salad, and red pepper sandwich (no mayo)
Half a honeydew melon

dinner
Starter: Vegetable soup and a bread roll

Main: Thick slab of fish in a light white wine sauce, with spinach and new potatoes

Dessert: Mousse of fromage frais, lemon and soaked dried fruit

Starter: Smoked salmon and lemon

Main: Wholegrain pasta with anchovies, sun-dried tomatoes and a little olive oil; fresh bread

Dessert: Frozen yogurt

ENERGY DRINKS, GELS, & BARS

Go into a sporting goods store and you are likely to see a range of energy-filled powders and packets aimed at runners. They are convenient—but do you need them? Here is the low-down on drinks, gels, and bars.

energy drinks
These are usually isotonic (easily digestible) and often contain sodium to speed up rehydration. Drinks made with complex carbohydrates (such as maltodextrin) can be mixed. They are good at high concentrations as a pre-run snack and during long runs. You can make an approximation at home by adding a pinch of salt to diluted fruit juice.

energy gels
Gels are syrupy, concentrated solutions of carbohydrate, which require no chewing and pack high energy counts for their small size. They are very convenient for long runs or races, although you need access to water as nearly all gels are indigestible without it.

energy bars
These are often little more than tasty low-fat snacks, although they are undeniably convenient. Like all solids, they are best not eaten on the run. Some contain protein, vitamins, and minerals, which makes them useful as recovery foods, but avoid any that contain more than 30 percent protein. Bagels or fig rolls are popular low-fat alternatives.

warming up, cooling down 1

Remember to jog slowly at the end of a hard run—it will aid muscle recovery and reduce the risk of injury.

Starting a run slowly enables your muscles to gradually lengthen and find their running shape, which will minimize injury risk. Allow 5–10 minutes of very easy running before you ease into your normal pace, plus some stretching if you are going to do some speedwork. If you run first thing in the morning, a couple of minutes of walking before even jogging is a good idea, as your cold body will have a very limited range of movement. At the end of brisk runs, do five minutes of easy running to reduce post-run soreness. And don't finish your runs with a sprint to the front door, as this fills your muscles with damaging waste products like lactic acid.

stretching

Tight muscles tear more easily than supple ones, so you should think of regular stretching as an insurance against injury. Follow this eight-stretch routine to keep flexible.

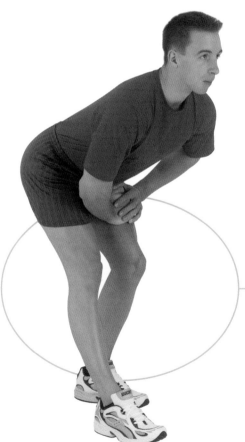

◄◄ hamstring stretch

Keep one leg straight. Bend the supporting leg at the knee and rest both hands on your thigh to support your weight. Now lean steeply forward from your hips, keeping your back straight. You will feel a stretch along the hamstring of your straight leg.

gluteal stretch

Sit down on the floor. Tuck the ankle of your right leg behind your left knee while using your left hand to hold your leg in position. Keep your right hand firmly on the floor for balance. You will feel a stretch in the muscles at the side of your buttocks. Repeat on the other side.

upper calf stretch

Keep your right leg straight, pushing the back heel into the ground. Lean forward and support your weight with your left leg. Gently lift up through your hips and feel a stretch on the calf of your extended leg. Repeat on the other side.

groin stretch

Holding the soles of your feet together, gently use your leg muscles to move your knees toward the ground. Maintaining a straight back and bringing your feet closer to your body intensifies the stretch.

warming up, cooling down 2

◀◀ lower calf stretch

Bend one leg, keeping the foot flat on the floor. You should feel a stretch in your lower calf.

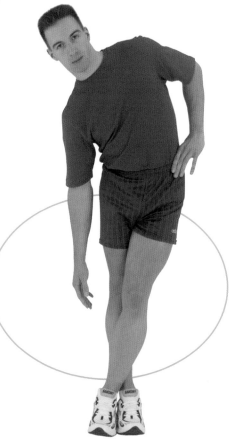

iliotibial stretch ▶▶

Place one foot around the other, with both feet flat on the ground. Keeping both legs straight, lean your hips away from your rear foot. You should feel a stretch down the outside of your leg and around your hip.

hip flexor stretch

Place one knee forward and extend your trailing leg behind. Rest your hands on your knee while keeping your hips squared forward and your upper body vertical. Do not slump forward, as this reduces the stretch.

quadricep stretch ▸▸

Balancing on one leg, pull up the other foot behind your body. Keep your body straight to maximize the stretch through the front of your leg.

resting

Your body needs rest in order to grow stronger; ignoring this truth is a fast route to injury and illness. Beginners should only run on alternate days at first. Experienced runners should aim to take at least one day off a week, one easy week per month, and ideally, one easy month a year. And all runners should avoid running hard days consecutively; even if you feel fine the day after a fast or long run, your recovering body will still be more susceptible to damage.

beating injury

treat injuries with RICE:

R—rest

Minimize movement and weight-bearing to the injured area. A couple of days off is an effective cure for many minor injuries.

I—ice

This reduces the damage from the swelling that accompanies strains and tears. Wrap an ice pack (or a bag of frozen peas) in a damp cloth and apply it firmly to the site of your injury for 15 minutes every hour, or as often as you can manage during the day. Taking nonsteroidal anti-inflammatory drugs such as ibuprofen also helps.

C—compression

A lightly elasticized bandage will help to reduce swelling further—but do not tie it so tightly that it restricts your circulation.

E—elevation

Keeping your leg raised will reduce blood circulation, which in the early stages of an injury will help to limit tissue damage.

achilles heel

Sports scientists have demonstrated that glucosamine supplements have a positive healing effect for many sufferers of Achilles pain.

Top-level runners know how to push through discomfort. They are also smart enough to pull up at the first sign of pain, as this indicates potential injury. It can take years to tell the difference between temporary discomfort and damage, but prompt action in the latter case will swing the balance between the need to take a couple of easy recovery days, and the need for weeks of total rest and medical treatment. Unlike discomfort, harmful pain tends to be localized and unfamiliar. If you do suffer leg pain, use our guide (see right) to diagnose the problem or illness.

self-treatment

When pain occurs on a run, stop, stretch lightly, then walk. If the pain then disappears, try a light jog, and then ease back into your run—otherwise cut your run short and return home at once. Once there, apply the RICE treatment (see left), which is effective first aid for most pains and sprains. Do not attempt to diagnose your own injury, and if the pain continues for more than two days, seek medical care—ideally, from a sports medicine specialist, physiotherapist, or osteopath.

a quick guide to five common injuries

injury	cause	treatment
1 Achilles pain	This is often caused by an excessive increase in speed or mileage, worn-out shoes, or by overpronation (see pages 14 and 95).	Ice and rest are the correct responses; when the swelling has disappeared, gently start to stretch the lower calf and ankle, and seek massage.
2 hamstring pain	Hamstring pains are often caused by a sudden or excessive increase in speed or mileage.	Rest, easy running, and massage are the best solutions to most hamstring tears. Avoid hill running and speedwork, ice the injury, and stretch regularly.
3 knee pain	Knee pain can be caused by a problem with the knee itself, or by a problem elsewhere. Check that muscle tightness isn't the source.	Stretch your iliotibial band, gluteal muscles and quadriceps, and mobilize your lower back. Ensure that your shoes are providing enough stability for your needs.
4 shinsplints	This pain along the front of the shins is caused by swelling of the muscles, tendons, or bone coverings. It is caused by overpronation, increased speed, and hard surfaces.	The RICE treatment will help. It is important to stretch and strengthen the shins, ankles, and calves. Avoid running on hard surfaces.
5 plantar fasciitis	Damage to the thick band that connects your heel to the base of your toes appears as pain at the base of your heel.	Stretch your calves and Achilles tendons. Also curl your toes and shift your weight to the outside of your foot as you stretch. A sports medicine specialist can help with massage and ultrasound treatment.

cross-training

Supplementing your running with other aerobic activities (such as cycling, swimming, or rowing) is an excellent way of boosting your fitness with minimal injury risk. Strength and flexibility training—such as weight training and yoga—also have great value. As well as helping with your general fitness, they should also make you a stronger runner. Up to a point, some coaches argue that the way to run better is to run more, but most runners would benefit from getting the maximum out of relatively low mileage and adding one or two good-quality cross-training sessions a week. You can use alternative training to replace one easy run a week, although there are definitely some running sessions—such as speedwork and long, slow runs—that cannot be adequately replicated through other activities.

play pool

Swimming is an excellent way of toning up just about every part of your body as well as giving yourself a good cardiovascular workout. It is also a good way of learning to regulate your breathing.

ten best ways to avoid injury

1	2	3	4	5
Don't stretch cold muscles	Wear good running shoes	Run on soft surfaces	Ease into your runs	Build mileage and speed gradually

cross-training to overcome injury ▶▶

hamstring pull

Rowing—Some gentle rowing sessions will extend the legs and gently stretch the damaged area. Over time, adding power strengthens the hamstring against future injury.

achilles tendinitis

Cycling—This provides excellent exercise as it stretches and strengthens your Achilles without impacting or twisting it.

Elliptical trainer—This is great for injury rehabilitation, as it involves no impact. Elliptical trainers allow you to run in a continuous motion that is a cross between cross-country skiing and stair climbing.

runner's knee

Brisk walking—Going for a walk straightens the leg, while exercising with a bent knee (as in cycling) can worsen the problem. Rowing and using an elliptical trainer can also help.

shinsplints

Cycling—Shinsplints can be eased through cycling, as it avoids putting pressure on the front of the lower leg. You can also try Nordic skiing and using an elliptical trainer.

plantar fascilitis

Cycling—Pedaling a bike can help to ease the tension on the underside of the foot, although it might be a little painful at first. You can also try rowing and using an elliptical trainer.

Cycling is good cardiovascular exercise and helps strengthen the legs and build stamina.

6	7	8	9	10
Don't run hard days consecutively	Don't ignore pain	Treat pain promptly	Return from illness or injury cautiously	Cross-train and strength train

motivation

Sometimes there are days when we would rather do anything other than go running. This will help you to get out and down the road.

challenging goals

Think of time spent running as an investment in a healthier, more relaxed, more fulfilled you. Your fitness will improve and you will be constantly reaching new goals. This will help you to keep up the momentum.

People give up when they become disappointed. And people get disappointed when their expectations differ from reality. That's why realistic goals are essential. If you are targeting your first race, simply aim to finish it as evenly and strongly as possible. If you are 47 and you have been running seriously for 20 years, don't aim to beat your all-time best this year, but try to beat the age-graded equivalent. And if you are a new runner, do not earmark a marathon as your first running target.

goals, now and later

Everyone needs a combination of long- and short-term aspirations to keep them on the move. The long-term targets give you a general direction; the short-term ones provide regular rewards and act as progress markers. Long-term goals are basically your underlying reasons for running. These could range from getting fit and losing weight to wanting to run a marathon. Your short-term goals should be more specific, such as losing five pounds in four weeks, or preparing for a 10K race. A realistic long-term goal might be to enter next year's marathon, or lose 20 lbs in weight, as well as markedly improve your general health, fitness, and sense of well-being.

ten best ways for staying motivated

1	2	3	4	5
Run free-form for a week Just head out at whatever pace and for however long your body wants to each day.	**...or quit for a week!** Especially effective if you are a regular runner. Soon you will be itching to train again.	**Keep a chart on your kitchen door** Put a tick in one column for each run you returned from feeling better.	**Find a running partner** Running with a partner will encourage you to stick to a routine.	**Set a goal** Whether it is to lose 5 lbs in a month or beat a personal best, it will motivate, focus, and reward you.

motivation for the beginner

When you are new to running keep in mind all the positive aspects of what running is doing for you. The rewards that come in the first few months of running are incredible. Your aerobic fitness will improve dramatically, you will shed surplus fat, and your body will firm up. As you progress, you will feel better all day as a result of being fit, and your sense of well-being will improve. These may seem like exaggerated boasts, but the experience of thousands of runners shows that running really does improve your health. When it is cold and wet outside and you shrink from the idea of running, just remind yourself of the benefits. And if you sometimes find it difficult to find the time to run, remember that it is an investment that will make your week more productive.

BANISH NEGATIVE THOUGHTS

Running is fantastic for the spirit: it is just you, your body, and your thoughts. The trouble begins when you start to believe that you are having a bad run. Here is how to squash those negative thoughts fast:

I'm slower than usual... Sometimes we have heavy, slow, breathless days—or weeks—for no apparent reason. When this happens, make the most of your run, at whatever pace feels right, and don't let a short period define the kind of runner you are. Your performances over a full month provide a better snapshot of your fitness.

I don't feel like a runner Try running tall—you will instantly feel sleeker and faster. Lift your spine up, broaden across your collarbone by dropping your shoulders down and back, and imagine that someone is gently pulling you forward and upward by a piece of string attached below your navel.

This run is going to take forever Break your runs down into sections—maybe 10-minute chunks, or laps of your local park. On the run, just focus on completing one section at a time (this is also a good mental trick for races). You will be surprised by how fast time passes.

6	7	8	9	10
Avoid comparisons If you must compare yourself with someone, make it a person who doesn't run.	**Keep it varied** Variety is the spice of life, so try a bit of cross-training (see pages 38–39).	**Help at a race** Witnessing other people's effort and achievement will remind you of the benefits of running.	**Buy some new shoes and clothes** This will help you to feel a renewed sense of purpose in your running.	**Join a club** Being encouraged or providing encouragement is a perfect enthusiasm-booster.

2

training schedules

One of the keys to enjoying running and making progress is to follow a schedule. This does not mean subjecting yourself to a strict regime or subscribing to detailed instructions and rules. It means giving yourself a working framework and goals to aim for. Saying to yourself, "I'm just going to run until I get tired," is the surest way of losing interest and giving up. Having a basic plan to follow will help you to keep motivated and achieve your goals.

This chapter provides day-by-day guides at six levels of ability, designed to help you achieve a wide range of training and racing goals safely and effectively. We also look at the simple principles of running that all runners should follow, whether or not they are following a schedule.

the four golden rules

1 build up slowly

You will avoid injury and improve more quickly in the long term by being patient about increasing your speed and mileage. Increase your weekly mileage by no more than three or four miles a week—less if you are a totally new runner. Ease gradually into speedwork, once you have built a base of low-intensity running. And avoid increasing speed and mileage at the same time.

2 take rest days

Your body needs time to recover— in fact it builds its fitness after rather than during your runs—so you should follow any day of fast or long running with a day of easy running or rest.

3 warm up and cool down

Your muscles, joints, ligaments, and tendons need time to ease into any run, because when you begin they will be short and tight. You should end any run with an easy jog and stretching.

4 pay attention to injury

Damage to your body will only get worse if you try to run through it. If you have persistent pain, rest and put ice on the sore area in the short-term, then seek a diagnosis from your local doctor, a specialist, or a good coach, and make every effort to rehabilitate the injury. Early treatment will bring a swifter recovery.

Follow the four basic training principles (see left) and you should be well on the way to being a happy, successful runner, whether or not you are following a training schedule.

Every run has a purpose, so if your routine demands a recovery day, hold back at a conversational pace. That will leave you fully recovered and eager for your next session. Conversely, when you do speedwork, you should end the session feeling that you have put in a genuinely tiring effort.

Now that you have read the four golden rules, you will realize that respect for your body is paramount (see pages 10–11 for more about running surfaces, pages 32–35 for warming up, and pages 36–37 for diagnosing and treating injuries). With these principles under your belt, you will be set for a lifetime of effective and supremely satisfying running.

training sessions

Most schedules also include a broad range of training sessions—some self-explanatory, some not so obvious. Variety is essential, both to keep yourself motivated, and to boost your strength and endurance. Here are the main types of sessions (see right).

training sessions

▶▶ brisk or threshold runs

Brisk runs equate to approximately half-marathon pace for experienced runners. Usually lasting from 20–40 minutes, which may be broken down into fast and slow segments, they are good for teaching your body to run for longer periods at speed.

▶▶ speedwork or intervals

Fast repetitions interspersed with rest periods—for example, 4 x 800 m with two-minute recoveries. They improve strength, speed, and form, and you don't have to be a "fast" runner to do them!

▶▶ long, slow runs

The key to building endurance, these are best done on the weekend or on a day off from work. Slow runs might progress to between one and three hours, depending on your goals. Time spent running is more important than speed.

▶▶ hill sessions

Speedwork on a slope, with a greater emphasis on power. You run hard uphill, jog down, and repeat. Distance and gradient variations are endless—a typical session would be 8–12 x 1 minute on a steep climb.

▶▶ fartlek

This is Swedish for "speed play," and is a free-form type of speedwork, in which you speed up at random intervals during a normal run.

how the training levels work

The training schedules in this section are divided into six levels of difficulty. The levels can be used alone or followed consecutively, and each includes higher mileage and intensity than the last. The first training level is purely for beginners. Its purpose is to build you up to running for 30 minutes nonstop. All the other levels feature a fitness-running schedule, and one or more racing schedules. The levels are arranged like this:

1 starter level	**2** starter level	**3** refresher level
pages 52–55	**pages 56–59**	**pages 60–63**
for complete beginners This includes four days a week of running and walking.	**for relatively new runners** This is for people who can run 30 minutes nonstop, three to four days a week.	**for lapsed runners** This is for those who can run 15–30 miles (25–50 km) over four to five days a week.
This level aims to enable you to run:	Use this schedule to train for:	Use this schedule to train for:
▦ 30 minutes nonstop.	▦ a 5K run (eight-week schedule).	▦ fitness (repeatable three- to four-week schedule).
It is a highly flexible schedule that lasts for about 10 weeks.	▦ longer runs and general fitness (repeatable, three- to four-week schedule).	▦ 10K runs (eight-week schedule).

96

be careful

Remember that all of the following schedules are guidelines only, and each schedule is intended for runners of the appropriate fitness level. Do not push yourself excessively, and listen to your body—if you feel any serious pain or discomfort, especially if you have not exercised regularly over the last five years, consult a doctor or sports injury specialist immediately.

4 intermediate level

pages 64–71

for regular runners
For those who can run 25–35 miles (30–58 km) over four to six days a week, and includes those who want to run up to a 4:15 marathon or 50-minute 10K race.

Use this schedule to train for:

- fitness (three- to four-week schedule).

- a 10K race/half-marathon (eight- to ten-week schedule).

- a full marathon (sixteen-week schedule).

5 upper level

pages 72–79

for experienced runners
This involves training five to six days a week, and includes those who want to run a 4:15–3:30 marathon, or a 50- to 40-minute 10K.

Use this schedule to train for:

- fitness (repeatable three- to four-week schedule).

- a 10K race/half marathon (eight- to ten-week schedule).

- a full marathon (sixteen-week schedule).

6 upper level

pages 80–87

for experienced runners
This is for runners who are training six to seven days a week, including those who want to run a 3:30–2:50 marathon, or a 40- to 34-minute 10K.

Use this schedule to train for:

- fitness (repeatable three- to four-week schedule).

- a 10K race/half-marathon (eight- to ten-week schedule).

- a full marathon (sixteen-week schedule).

basic heart-rate training

A heart-rate monitor can help to ensure that you do not work too hard—or take it too easy!—in training sessions. A basic model costs less than a pair of cheap running shoes, and it is very easy to use (see page 22 for more about this). Depending on your training session, your target heart rate will be anywhere between 60 percent and 95 percent of your normal working range.

To know your target heart rate, you will need to know your maximum. If you are more than 20 percent overweight or a beginner, it is best to use the approximate formula below to estimate your maximum:

214 – (0.8 x age) for men
209 – (0.9 x age) for women

For example, a 30 year old man might have a rate of:

0.8 x 30 = 24
214 - 24 = 190

training at the right rate	find your training zone like this:
There are three broad training zones: **60–75 percent** EASY **75–85 percent** MODERATE **85–95 percent** HARD **BUT... DO NOT FALL VICTIM TO A COMMON MISCONCEPTION:** These are not percentages of your overall maximum heart rate, they are percentages based on your *working* heart rate. It makes a big practical difference to a regular runner. The calculation is easy to do, but it takes more explanation than most gyms are prepared to give.	**1** Calculate your maximum heart rate (see above), for example, 206. **2** Calculate your resting heart rate. This should be done lying still, soon after you wake up. For example, this might be 56. **3** Subtract the resting rate from the maximum. This figure is your working heart rate. For example: 206–56 = 150 **4** Take the percentage of your working heart rate that you are aiming for—for example, 60 percent for an easy run is 150 x 0.60 = 90—and add it to your resting heart rate (90+56 = 146). The final figure is your personal target heart rate for the session.

run for the max

Unfortunately, for five to ten percent of the population this figure can be wrong by up to 24 beats per minute. It is much better to find your maximum through running. Do this by warming up with some stretching, then running as fast as you can at an even pace for three minutes (ideally on a treadmill), then resting with two minutes of gentle running, then repeating your three-minute maximal run. During your second run you should get a higher maximum heart rate than with any other method—though use your heart-rate monitor to take readings throughout, as your heart rate may peak before the run is completed.

Note that a heart-rate monitor is little use for pacing intervals of less than 1000 m; the figures above 85 percent are guides to what you can expect to reach at the end of each repetition.

If the target pace seems way too slow...
■ You may not be using an accurate maximum heart rate (if you have estimated it). Add 12 beats to your theoretical maximum and try the calculations again.
■ You may be using percentages of your maximum heart rate rather than your working heart rate (see left).

sample sessions

60 PERCENT
Recovery run—dead slow. Although slow, recovery runs are crucial. Takes 30 mins.

60 to 70 PERCENT
Long, slow run—up to 65 percent the body is teaching itself to burn fat as fuel (useful for marathons).
Takes anything from one to three hours.

75 to 85 PERCENT
Fartlek—speed play (moderate-paced runs with random fast bursts). Takes 30–60 mins.
Undulating route—peak at 85 percent on the climbs. Takes 30–90 minutes.

85 PERCENT
Anaerobic threshold run (or "tempo run"). Approximately ten-mile (16 km) to half-marathon race pace.
Sample session: 1.5 miles at 60 percent, then 15–20 minutes at 85 percent, then 1.5 miles at 60 percent.

85 to 90 PERCENT
Approximately 5K to 10K pace.
Sample sessions: 6 x 800 m peaking at 90 percent in each repetition; or 5 x 2000 m peaking at 85 percent in each repetition.

95 PERCENT
Peak heart rate at 400 m interval pace (not full-out race pace). Sample session: 12 x 400 m with 200 m jog recoveries, making sure recovery heart rate drops to at least 70 percent.

stronger, faster, quicker

Speedwork (also known as "intervals" or "repetitions") is the single best way to become a stronger, faster, more confident runner. A weekly session will pay dividends whether you are a twelve-minute miler or an advanced five-minute miler.

Once you have progressed to running 30–40 minutes or more, three or four times a week, you can think about turning one of your sessions into speedwork. This will be hard work, but you will see the benefits within days:

your fitness levels will increase rapidly, and your normal running will become easier and more enjoyable.

types of speedwork

All speedwork includes periods of hard running interspersed with rest. Beyond that, the variations are infinite. You can do speedwork on a measured track or stretch of grass, though exact distances are not essential. The rest interval (during which you stand, jog, or walk) can vary according to the

purpose of the session—short distances and/or long rests are best for building pure speed, while longer distances and/or shorter rests will build speed and endurance. A good rule is to rest for the amount of time it took to run the effort. Typical sessions might be 8 x 400 m; 4 x 800 m; 3 x 1200 m; or 200 m, 400 m, 800 m, 1200 m, 800 m, 400 m, 200 m (this is called a pyramid session). You can also run by time rather than distance—for example, 8 x 90 seconds, or 4 x 4 minutes.

how hard should you run?

As long as you are making a greater effort than your normal training pace, you are doing speedwork. Once you are used to this style of training, you should be aiming to run hard but evenly—your last repetition in a session should be as strong as your first, without leaving you feeling as though you could have gone faster.

As well as improving your fitness enormously, speedwork also teaches you the valuable art of pacing yourself.

1

starter level

This level is for those who are completely new to running. The purpose of the schedule is to build you up to running 30 minutes nonstop. Once you have completed this level you can definitely think of yourself as a "real" runner, and if you want to, you will have the ability to get to the finishing line of a 5K race. (Once you can run 30 minutes nonstop, there is a specific schedule in Level 2 (pages 58–59) for training to run slightly harder in a 5K.) If you are fit already, you will not need to start at the

beginning of this schedule, and you will probably be able to advance safely through it faster than we suggest (see left, "Fit Already?"). Either way, be patient, and try to run slower than you think you need to. You may well have the heart, lungs and power to run quickly, but your muscles, joints, and tendons won't be adapted to running yet, and they are especially susceptible to injury in these early stages. Think of these slow weeks as an investment in what could develop into a lifetime of fulfilling, injury-free running.

fit already?

Some people—even if they do not regularly run or exercise—will find that they can run 30 minutes nonstop on day one. Others will adapt very quickly to the training program and be ready to build up sessions faster than the schedules suggest. It is only natural: we all have different levels of residual fitness and some bodies are quicker than others to adapt to the mechanical demands of running. In all cases, however, you should be aiming to run gradually longer rather than faster at this stage, otherwise you will risk injury. Follow the suggestions ("If you...") on pages 53 and 55 if you are already reasonably fit.

level 1 schedule

Repeat each session four times a week. Try not to train on consecutive days at this stage, and remember that by run, we mean jog easily at a pace that would let you continue a conversation (about 60–70 percent of your working heart rate—see pages 48–49). Your walk breaks should be brisk and purposeful. If you need to repeat a week, drop back a week, or alternate our suggested sessions with easier ones over two weeks instead of a week, then it is perfectly OK to do so.

Finally, if you're not ready to exercise for a full 30 minutes yet—especially if you are more than 20 percent above your ideal weight—spend two, three, or more weeks walking briskly for 20–30 minutes, four days a week. It is the best way to prepare your legs for running, it is good cardiovascular exercise, and it will get you used to having a routine.

WEEK

1
Run 2 minutes, walk 2 minutes.
Do this seven times per session.

WEEK

2
Run 4 minutes, walk 2 minutes.
Do this five times per session.

WEEK

3
Run 6 minutes, walk 2 minutes.
Do this four times per session.

week 3—how's it going?

Are you running at a conversational pace? Are you feeling ready to run again after the walk breaks? Are you staying free of aches and pains? Yes? Good—you're ready to progress to Week 4. If you answered "no" to any of these questions, see "It's Too Hard" (page 54). However, if by running at a conversational pace you are finding the runs supremely unchallenging, and your body is free of aches and pains, move on to Week 6.

WEEK

4
Run 8 minutes, walk 2 minutes.
Do this three times per session.

WEEK

5
Run 6 minutes, walk 2 minutes, run 10 minutes,
walk 2 minutes, run 10 minutes, walk 2 minutes

WEEK

6
Run 10 minutes, walk 1 minute.
Do this three times per session.

week 6—how's it going?

If you are finding it a struggle to get to the end of a 10-minute run, do not worry—just drop down to Week 5, or even Week 4, until your body tells you it is ready to progress further. If you are finding this too easy, skip Week 7, but progress normally through Weeks 8, 9, and 10. Patience is essential to build your running foundation and avoid injury.

If you...

can run 30 minutes nonstop
Spend the next four weeks doing three or four easy runs of 20–40 minutes a week. After that, you are ready to start the schedules in Level 2—just allow at least two more weeks before you begin speedwork.

If you...

can run 10–15 minutes nonstop without getting out of breath
Begin the Level 1 schedules at a week that demands repeated runs of two to four minutes less than your comfortable limit. If it is too hard, don't be ashamed to drop back a week or two.

1 starter level

it's too hard!

Far too many new runners give up because they try to run too hard, too soon. They feel they should be progressing faster—or they simply get injured—and then deny themselves a lifetime of fitness because they decide they are not cut out to be a runner. Have faith in yourself! Unless you have a serious medical problem, you can develop into a runner—at whatever speed is right for you. Just look at the success stories of obese people who more than halved their weight by building up through a combination of walking and running. Or cancer patients who defied the odds to start— or continue—running. Or amputees, or 75-year-olds, who did the same.

Do not be ashamed to slow down. If you are struggling, drop back to a week in the schedules that leaves you truly comfortable—even if it is Week 1—and just repeat it again and again until you (not anyone else) feel that you are ready to move up. Then repeat the next week as many times as you need to, and so on. Also, try to find a partner to join you; try to run on soft surfaces; and stretch afterward to minimize aches and pains (see pages 40–41 for more motivational ideas).

WEEK 7
Run 13 minutes, walk 1 minute, run 14 minutes, walk 1 minute.

WEEK 8
Run 15 minutes, walk 1 minute, run 16 minutes, walk 1 minute.

WEEK 9
Run 17 minutes, walk 1 minute, run 18 minutes, walk 1 minute.

week 9—how's it going?

By now you might be itching to get on to Week 10 and progress through the final longer runs to your 30-minute target. If you are not suffering any aches and pains, and you have cruised easily through the last week's runs, then you should be fine to do just that. If you are not quite so confident, but you do feel ready to start Week 10, feel free to spread the week's five sessions over two weeks instead, alternating each session with easy run/walk days.

I get a stitch or stomach cramp

Stitches are sharp pains just below the ribcage, caused by cramp in the stomach wall. Here is what you can do to beat them:

■ If you get a stitch on your right side, keep exhaling hard every time your left foot lands on the ground. If the stitch is on the left, breathe out hard when your right foot lands.

■ Breathe deeply from your stomach while running with your hands on top of your head and your elbows tucked back.

■ Hold a deep breath for 15 seconds while you continue to run.

■ Stop and touch your toes a few times.

■ The most extreme method is to push one fist under your ribcage with your other arm, then bend over to almost 90 degrees while continuing to run for 10 steps.

Stomach cramp can also be caused by eating or drinking too soon before a run. This is a very individual matter—some people can run comfortably 20 or 30 minutes after having a light snack; others need to avoid food completely for three or four hours. (See pages 26–27 for more about eating before you run.)

If you...

want to progress faster through the schedules

As long as your body remains completely pain free and you can continue to run at a conversational pace, you can miss every third week in the schedule. Alternatively, run four days a week taking alternate days from an easier and a harder week (for example, Weeks 2 and 3), then move up to alternate days from more difficult weeks (for example, Weeks 4 and 5).

WEEK

10   DAILY SCHEDULE

DAY 1: Run 9 minutes, walk 1 minute, run 21 minutes.

DAY 2: Run 7 minutes, walk 1 minute, run 23 minutes.

DAY 3: Run 5 minutes, walk 1 minute, run 25 minutes.

DAY 4:: Run 3 minutes, walk 1 minute, run 27 minutes.

DAY 5: Run 30 minutes!

57

2 starter level 4 weeks, repeatable

This level is for runners of all speeds, but it assumes that you can run nonstop for 30 minutes. It consists of a fitness-running schedule and a first 5K race schedule. If you cannot run for 30 minutes nonstop yet, build up using the program in Level 1. If you have never done any running before and yet your natural fitness allows you to run for 30 minutes straight away, resist the temptation to speed up until you have been running for at least six weeks. Instead, spend the next four weeks doing three or four easy runs a week, each lasting 20–40 minutes. After that, you can start the schedules in Level 2— just allow at least two more weeks before you begin speedwork.

level 2 fitness schedule

FOUR WEEKS, REPEATABLE

Before you start you should be able to run 30 minutes nonstop, three to four days per week.

To use the fitness schedule, first follow the main sessions. If you want to progress when you have comfortably completed the first four-week cycle, repeat the schedule with the variations.

If you suffer any aches and pains, do not hesitate to replace a long or hard run with a shorter or easier one. Remember that even slow runs will build your fitness at this stage. Running regularly, and within your limits, is the most important thing.

WEEK		MONDAY	TUESDAY	
1		rest	10 mins slow (see p. 95); then 4 x 1 min brisk (see p. 95) with 2-min jog recoveries (see p. 95); then 10 mins slow	
CYCLE **2**			add one repetition	
2		rest	10 mins slow, then 20 mins fartlek (see p. 95), then 10 mins slow	
CYCLE **2**			add 5 mins fartlek	
3		rest	10 mins slow; then 4 x 90 secs fast (see p. 95) with 2.5-min jog recoveries; then 10 mins slow	
CYCLE **2**			add 30 secs to each effort	
4		rest	10 mins slow; then 2 x 4 mins brisk, with 4-min jog recoveries	
CYCLE **2**			add 1 min to each effort	

week 4—how's it going?

Be sure to take your time. If you are becoming frequently tired, or if you have persistent aches and pains, ease off the pace and do not hesitate to replace a long or hard run with a shorter or easier one.

If you have reached the end of Week 4 with no problems, and you want to get ready for level 3, progress to Cycle 2. Otherwise, repeat the first cycle for as long as you wish, or simply until you feel comfortable with it.

What pace?

At this stage, most of your runs should be at a pace that allows you to hold a conversation. The aim is to build up your fitness and endurance, and that means working to increase the amount of time you can comfortably spend running. If in doubt, slow down, and take occasional one-minute walk breaks on the longer runs.

Your schedules contain one run a week that includes faster-paced running (speedwork). Do not run yourself to a standstill—the aim is to run quickly but evenly, so that you can run your last burst as fast as your first.

WEDNESDAY	THURSDAY	FRIDAY	SATURDAY	SUNDAY
rest	25–35 mins slow	rest	25–35 mins slow	35 mins slow
	add 5 mins if desired			add 10 mins
rest	25–35 mins slow	rest	25–35 mins slow	40 mins slow
	add 5 mins if desired			add 15 mins
rest	25–35 mins slow	rest	25–35 mins slow	45 mins slow
	add 5 mins if desired			add 15 mins
rest	25–35 mins slow	rest	25–35 mins slow	50 mins slow
	add 5 mins if desired			add 15 mins

2

5K schedule 6–8 weeks

Before you start this schedule you should be able to run 30 minutes nonstop, three to four days a week.

optional 2 week build-up

week one	week two
MONDAY	**MONDAY**
rest	rest
TUESDAY	**TUESDAY**
25 mins slow	25 mins slow, incorporating six sets of 20–40 seconds faster-paced running
WEDNESDAY	**WEDNESDAY**
rest	rest
THURSDAY	**THURSDAY**
20–30 mins slow	20–30 mins slow
FRIDAY	**FRIDAY**
rest	rest
SATURDAY	**SATURDAY**
20–25 mins slow	20–25 mins steady
SUNDAY	**SUNDAY**
30–35 mins slow	30–35 mins slow

WEEK	MONDAY	TUESDAY	
1	rest	10 mins slow (see p. 95); then 4–6 x 1 min brisk (see p. 95) with 2-min jog recoveries (see p. 95); then 10 mins slow	
2	rest	10 mins slow, then 20–30 mins fartlek (see p. 95), then 10 mins slow	
3	rest	10 mins slow; then 4–6 x 90 secs with 2.5-min jog recoveries; then 10 mins slow	
4	rest	10 mins slow, then 20 mins fartlek, then 10 mins slow	
5	rest	10 mins slow; then 3–4 x 3 mins brisk with 3-min jog recoveries; then 10 mins slow	
6	rest	25 mins slow, incorporating 6 x 20–40 secs faster-paced running sets (see p. 95)	

week 4—how's it going?

You can give yourself a rough 5K time target on the basis of this week's one-mile time trial:

10 mins = 34 mins (with some walking)
9 mins = 31 mins   7 mins = 24 mins
8 mins = 27 mins   6 mins = 20 mins

If you have reached the end of Week 4 with no problems, and you want to get ready for Level 3, progress to Cycle 2. Otherwise, repeat the first cycle until you feel comfortable with it.

WEDNESDAY	THURSDAY	FRIDAY	SATURDAY	SUNDAY
rest	20–30 mins slow	rest	20–25 mins steady (see p. 95)	30–40 mins slow
rest	20–30 mins slow	rest	20–25 mins steady	35–45 mins slow
rest	25–35 mins slow	rest	25–30 mins steady	40–50 mins slow
rest	10 mins slow, then stretch (see pp. 32–35); then 1 measured mile (timed), fast; then 10 mins slow	rest	20–25 mins slow	45–55 mins slow
rest	25–35 mins slow	rest	25–30 mins steady	35–45 mins slow
rest	20–25 mins slow	rest	15–20 mins slow or rest	5K race

how's it going? ⌃

3

refresher level 4 weeks, repeatable

This level is for those who have built up to running 15–25 miles (25–40 km) over four to five days a week. It contains a fitness running schedule and a 10K schedule, both of which can accommodate a wide range of runners. If you are planning to follow the 10K schedule, build up with a few weeks of running at least 15–18 miles (25–30 km) before you start. The 10K training mileages increase from week to week, and the better your training base, the better you will adapt to this. You will reap maximum fitness benefits with minimum injury risk by patiently building your weekly mileage by just two or three miles a week.

level 3 fitness schedule

FOUR WEEKS, REPEATABLE

Before you begin you should be able to run 30–35 minutes nonstop, over four to five days per week.

To use the fitness schedule, first follow the main sessions. If you want to progress when you have comfortably completed the first four-week cycle, repeat the schedule and variations with Cycle 2. If you suffer any aches and pains, do not hesitate to replace a long or hard run with a shorter or easier one. Remember that even slow runs will build your fitness at this stage. Running regularly, and within your limits, is more important than increasing your speed.

WEEK	MONDAY	TUESDAY
1	rest	10 mins jog (see p. 95); then 4 x 2 mins (or 400 m) fast (see p. 95), with 2-min jog recoveries; then 10 mins jog
CYCLE 2		add one repetition
2	rest	10 mins slow, then 20 mins fartlek (see p. 95), 10 mins slow
CYCLE 2		add 5 mins fartlek
3	rest	10 mins slow; then 1 min, 2 mins, 4 mins, 2 mins, 1 min (or 200 m, 400 m, 800 m, 400 m, 200 m) fast, with equal time recoveries; then 10 mins slow
CYCLE 2		add 30 secs to each effort
4	rest	10 mins slow; then 3 x 4 mins (or 800 m) brisk, with 4-min jog recoveries
CYCLE 2		add 1 min to each effort

week 4—how's it going?

Be sure to take your time. If you are becoming frequently tired, or if you have persistent aches and pains, don't hesitate to replace a long or hard run with a shorter or easier one. Slow runs are particularly good for building your fitness at this stage. It is most important to run regularly, and within your limits.

If you have reached the end of Week 4 with no problems, and you want to get ready for Level 4 (page 64), progress to Cycle 2. Otherwise, repeat the first cycle for as long as you wish. At the end of Cycle 2, either repeat the cycle again or move up to Level 4. It is your choice!

WEDNESDAY	THURSDAY	FRIDAY	SATURDAY	SUNDAY
rest or 25–35 mins slow (see p. 95)	25–35 mins slow	rest	25–35 mins slow	35–45 mins slow
	add 5 mins if desired			add 10 mins
rest or 25–35 mins slow	25–35 mins slow	rest	25–35 mins slow	40–50 mins slow
	add 5 mins if desired			add 15 mins
rest or 30–40 mins slow	25–35 mins slow	rest	25–35 mins slow, with strides (see p. 95)	45–55 mins slow
	add 5 mins if desired			add 15 mins
rest or 30–40 mins slow	10 mins slow, then 15–25 mins fartlek	rest	25–35 mins slow, with strides	50–60 mins slow
	add 5 mins if desired			add 15 mins

WHAT TIME OF DAY SHOULD I TRAIN? There is no right or wrong time to run, but it is good to get into a routine so that going for a run becomes an integral part of your day. Many runners get into the habit of training before breakfast—it leaves the rest of the day free and gives a sense of achievement before half of your neighbors are awake. Others find that lunchtime or evening suits their bodies better—especially for speedwork. Either way, try to have a plan for your week ahead—and even schedule runs into your diary if necessary (that way, you will be more likely to stick to them). If you can, try running at least part of the way to or from work sometimes. It is an ideal way to fit in some mileage with a minimal time cost (provided you can wash at the office!).

refresher level—first 10K

Before you begin this schedule you should be able to run 18–25 miles (30–40 km) over four or five days a week.

NOTE: Throughout the schedules, "miles" are referred to as "M."

week 3—how's it going?

You can give yourself a rough 10K time target on the basis of your one-mile time trial:

10+ mins = 70 mins (with some walking)
9 mins = 65 mins
8 mins = 58 mins
7 mins = 51 mins
6 mins = 43 mins

If you finished in less than seven minutes you have good natural speed. You could consider jumping to Week 4 of the 10K schedule in Level 5 (page 74), but our recommendation is to see how well you can do on the relatively low mileage in this level, or the low end of Level 4, before progressing.

TRAINING WITH FASTER (OR SLOWER) FRIENDS
Different-paced runners won't be able to do all of their training together, but you can coordinate all or part of some runs so that the faster runner enjoys a scheduled slow day while the slower runner has a tempo run. Speed sessions are a great opportunity to combine abilities, as they are usually based around a loop, so the slower runner can take shortcuts. Hill work can be used, too—both runners set off at the same time, the faster runner beginning from further down the slope.

WEEK	MONDAY	TUESDAY
1	rest	1.5 M jog (see p. 95); then 4 x 400 m fast (see p. 95), with 2-min recoveries (see p. 95); 1.5 M jog
2	rest	1.5 M jog; then 4 x 600 m fast, with 2.5-min recoveries; then 1.5 M jog
3	rest	1.5 M jog; then 1 M measured time-trial; then 1.5 M jog
4	rest	2 M jog; then 200 m, 400 m, 800 m, 400 m, 200 m with recoveries half as long as the efforts; then 2 M jog
5	rest	1.5 M jog; then 4 x 400 m fast, with 3-min recoveries; then 1.5 M jog
6	rest	2 M jog; then 1 M measured time-trial; then 2 M jog
7	rest	1.5 M jog; 3 x 1000 m brisk, with 4-min recoveries; then 1.5 M jog
8	rest	1.5 M jog; then 5 x 400 m fast, with 2-min recoveries; 1.5 M jog

week 6—how's it going?

Don't worry if last week's time trial was not faster than the first one. It doesn't mean you are not fitter—after all, your last three weeks' training has definitely had a positive effect. But do use last week's time trial result as a pace guide for the 10K. If you can, find out whether your race course will be marked in miles or kilometers, then divide your target time by 6.2 to find your target pace per mile (or 10 to find your target pace per kilometer). Set off on the race day at your target pace, then speed up in the last 2 miles (3 kilometers) if you feel strong.

WEDNESDAY	THURSDAY	FRIDAY	SATURDAY	SUNDAY
rest or 3–4 M slow (see p. 95)	4–5 M steady (see p. 95)	rest	10 mins slow, 10 mins brisk (see p. 95), 10 mins slow	4 M slow
rest or 3–4 M slow	4–5 M steady	rest	10 mins slow, then 25 mins fartlek (see p. 95)	5 M slow
rest or 3–4 M slow	4–5 M steady	rest	1.5 M jog; then 3 x 800 m fast, with 3-min recoveries; then 1.5 M jog	6 M slow

◀◀ how's it going?

rest or 3–4 M slow	4–5 M steady	rest	10 mins slow, 15–20 mins brisk, 10 mins slow	4 M slow
rest or 4–5 M slow	5–6 M steady	rest	10 mins slow, then 30 mins fartlek	6 M slow
rest or 4–5 M slow	5–6 M steady	rest	2 M jog; then 8 x 1-min steep hill climbs, jogging back down; then 2 M jog	7 M slow

▲ how's it going?

rest or 5–6 M slow	6–7 M steady	rest	10 mins slow, 10 mins brisk, 10 mins slow	8 M slow
rest	3–4 M steady	rest	25 mins slow, inc. strides (see p. 95)	**10K race**

intermediate level

4

This level is for you if you have built up to running 20–30 miles (32–48 km) over four to five days a week. It assumes that your typical training pace is 9- to 11-minute miling, though it is entirely suitable for faster runners who want to get the best out of lower mileages.

This level contains a fitness schedule, a 10K and half-marathon schedule, and a marathon schedule. The half- and full-marathon schedules are ideal if you are planning your first race at those distances, and could take an average runner to times of up to 1:50 and 4:15 respectively. If you have built up from Level 3, you should be able to ease comfortably into the Level 4 training. If you have only just reached the minimum mileage for Level 4, aim to follow at least one cycle of the Level 4 fitness schedule (see right) before beginning any of the race schedules.

To use the fitness schedule, first follow the main sessions. To progress, repeat the schedule, incorporating the variations as outlined in Cycle 2.

SPEEDWORK GUIDE
Your speedwork pace should be one that you can maintain strongly but evenly. You can expect to be capable of averaging the following times:

- If you can run 60 minutes for 10K:
  400 m = 2:05
  800 m = 4:20
  1200 m = 7:10

- If you can run 55 minutes for 10K:
  400 m = 1:55
  800 m = 4:00
  1200 m = 6:35

- If you can run 50 minutes for 10K:
  400 m = 1:45
  800 m = 3:40
  1200 m = 6:00

WEEK	MONDAY
1	rest
CYCLE **2**	
2	rest
CYCLE **2**	
3	rest
CYCLE **2**	
4	rest
CYCLE **2**	

week 4—how's it going?

Be sure to take your time. If you are becoming frequently tired, or if you have persistent aches and pains, don't hesitate to replace a long or hard run with a shorter or easier one. Remember that even slow runs will build your fitness at this stage. Running regularly, and within your limits, is the most important thing. If you have reached the end of Week 4 without problems, and you want to get ready for Level 5, progress to Cycle 2. Otherwise, repeat the first cycle for as long as you wish. At the end of Cycle 2, either repeat the cycle or move up to Level 5.

TUESDAY	WEDNESDAY	THURSDAY	FRIDAY	SATURDAY	SUNDAY
10 mins jog (see p. 95); 5 x 2 mins (or 400 m) fast (see p. 95), with 2-min jog recoveries (see p. 95); 10 mins jog	rest or 25–35 mins slow (see p. 95)	25–35 mins slow	rest	25–35 mins slow	40–50 mins slow
add one repetition		add 5–10 mins			add 10 mins
10 mins slow; 20–25 mins fartlek (see p. 95); then 10 mins slow	rest or 25–35 mins slow	25–35 mins slow	rest	25–35 mins slow	45–55 mins slow
add 5 mins fartlek		add 5–10 mins			add 15 mins
10 mins slow; then 1 min, 2 mins, 3 mins, 5 mins, 3 mins, 2 mins, 1 min (or 200 m, 400 m, 600 m, 1000 m, 600 m, 400 m, 200 m) fast, with equal-time recoveries; then 10 mins slow	rest or 30–40 mins slow	25–35 mins slow	rest	30–40 mins slow, with strides (see p. 95)	50–55 mins slow
add 30 secs to each effort		add 5–10 mins			add 15 mins
10 mins slow; then 3 x 4 mins (or 800 m) brisk (see p. 95), with 3-min jog recoveries	rest or 30–40 mins slow	10 mins slow, then 20–30 mins fartlek	rest	30–40 mins slow, with strides	Race 5–10K, or run 55–65 mins slow
add 1 min to each effort		add 5–10 mins			Race 5–10K, or add 15 mins

⌃ how's it going?

4

10K & half–marathon schedules

(APPROX 50 MINS +/- 10K; 1:50+ HALF-MARATHON)

HALF–MARATHON RUNNERS:
The variations to your schedule are the figures in [brackets].

WEEK	MONDAY	TUESDAY	WEDNESDAY	
1	rest	1.5 M jog (see p. 95); then 5 x 400 m, with 2-min recoveries (see p. 95); then 1.5 M jog	rest or 4–5 M slow (see p. 95)	
2	rest	1.5 M jog; then 5 x 600 m, with 2.5-min recoveries; then 1.5 M jog [2 x 1200 m with 3-min recoveries]	rest or 4–5 M slow	
3	rest	1.5 M jog; then 1 M measured time trial; then 1.5 M jog	rest or 4–5 M slow [or 5–6 M]	
4	rest	2 M jog; then 200 m, 400 m, 600 m, 800 m, 600 m, 400 m, 200 m fast, with recoveries half as long as the efforts; then 2 M jog	rest or 4 M slow [or 5 M]	
5	rest	1.5 M jog; then 5 x 800 m, with 3-min recoveries; then 1.5 M jog	rest or 4 M slow [or 5 M]	
6	rest	2 M jog; then 1 M measured time-trial; then 2 M jog [do Saturday's session]	rest or 5–6 M slow [or 6–7 M]	

Before you start you should be able to run 20–30 miles
(30–45 km) over four to five days a week.

THURSDAY	FRIDAY	SATURDAY	SUNDAY
5–6 M steady (see p. 95)	rest	10 mins slow, 10 mins brisk (see p. 95), 10 mins slow	5 M slow [6 M]
5–6 M steady	rest	10 mins slow, then 30 mins fartlek (see p. 95)	6 M slow [7 M]
5–6 M steady	rest	1.5 M jog; then 4 x 800 m, with 3-min recoveries; then 1.5 M jog	7 M slow [8 M]

how's it going? ▶▶

THURSDAY	FRIDAY	SATURDAY	SUNDAY
5–6 M steady	rest	10 mins slow, 20–25 mins brisk, 10 mins slow	5 M slow [6 M]
5–6 M steady	rest	10 mins slow, then 35 mins fartlek	7 M slow [8 M]
6–7 M steady	rest	2 M jog; then 10 x 1-min steep hill climbs, with jogs back down; then 2 M jog [3 M slow, inc. strides]	8 M slow [10K race]

how's it going? ▶▶

week 3—how's it going?

You can give yourself a rough 10K time target on the basis of Tuesday's one-mile time trial:
10+ mins = 70+ mins (with walking)
9 mins = 65 mins
8 mins = 58 mins
7 mins = 51 mins
6 mins = 43 mins

It is harder to predict half-marathon times from a mile run, but they potentially equate to 2:50+, 2:33, 2:15, 1:57 and 1:39 respectively.
    If you ran in less than seven minutes you have good natural speed. You could consider jumping to Week 4 of the schedules in Level 5 (page 72), but before you can safely make the transition, you will need to gradually build up to 30 miles a week.

week 6—how's it going?

10K runners: Use last week's time trial result as a pace guide for your 10K. Find out whether your race course will be marked in miles or kilometers, then divide your target time by 6.2 to find your target pace per mile, or 10 to find your target pace per kilometer. Set off on race day at your target pace, then speed up for the last 2 miles (3 km).

Half-marathoners: The 10K race should give you a good feeling for a half-marathon target:
60 mins = 2:20
54 mins = 2:05
48 mins = 1:50
42 mins = 1:35
40 mins = 1:30.
If you have aches or pains, don't push through them (see pages 36–37).

weeks 7, 8, 9, 10 ▶▶

4

10K & half-marathon schedules: continued

WEEK	MONDAY	TUESDAY	WEDNESDAY
7	rest	1.5 M jog; then 4 x 1000 m, with 3-min recoveries; then 1.5 M jog	rest or 5–6 M slow [or 6–7 M]
8	rest	1.5 M jog; then 6 x 400 m, with 2-min recoveries; then 1.5 M jog [2–3 x 1 M, with 4-min recoveries]	rest or 5–6 M slow [6–7 M slow]
9	rest	2 M jog; then 200 m, 400 m, 600 m, 800 m, 600 m, 400 m, 200 m, with recoveries half as long as the efforts; then 2 M jog	rest or 5–6 M slow
10	rest	1 M jog, then 1 M brisk, then 2 M jog	rest or 4 M slow

HALF-MARATHON RUNNERS: The variations to your schedule are the figures in [brackets].

half-marathon only

marathon schedule (4:15+)

Before you start you should be able to run 20–30 miles over four to five days a week, with regular long runs of at least 6–7 miles. If you cannot do that yet, you may still have the potential to complete a marathon. Replace the Tuesday sessions with easy runs, and plan to take one-minute walk breaks every 5–10 minutes during your long Sunday runs (this is an effective marathon-day plan, too). Add strides or an easy version of the speedwork on Tuesday only if you feel comfortable.

WEEK	MONDAY	TUESDAY	
1	rest	1 M jog; then 2–3 x 800 m, with 2-min recoveries; then 1 M jog	
2	rest	1–1.5 M jog; then 2 x 1200 m, with 4-mins recovery; then 1–1.5 M jog	
3	rest	1 M jog; then 800 m, 1200 m, 800 m, with 4-min recoveries; then 1 M jog	
4	rest	1–2 M jog; then 6 x 400 m, with 2-min recoveries; then 1–2 M jog	

THURSDAY	FRIDAY	SATURDAY	SUNDAY
7–8 M steady	rest	10 mins slow, 15 mins brisk, 10 mins slow	9 M slow [9–10 M]
4–5 M steady [6–7 M]	rest	30 mins slow, inc. strides [10 mins slow, then 30 mins fartlek]	10K race [10–11 M slow]
5–6 M steady	rest	10 mins slow, 10 mins brisk, 10 mins slow	7–8 M slow
5 M easy fartlek (see p. 95)	rest	rest or 3 M easy	**half-marathon race**

WEDNESDAY	THURSDAY	FRIDAY	SATURDAY	SUNDAY
rest or 5 M slow	5–6 M slow	rest	5 M slow, off-road	5–7 M slow
rest or 5 M slow	1 M slow, then 3–4 M steady, then 1 M slow	rest	4–5 M slow, off-road	7–9 M slow
rest or 5 M slow	2 M slow, then 1–2 M brisk, then 2 M slow	rest	5–6 M slow, off-road	8–11 M slow
rest or 5 M slow	5–7 M relaxed fartlek	rest	3–4 M slow, off-road	10K race

how's it going? ▸▸

weeks 5–16 ▶▶

4

marathon schedule (4:15+)

week 4— how's it going?

Your aim so far is to grow comfortable with increasing mileage, so do not worry about your speed. If you ran 10K in less than 50 minutes, however, you have the potential to beat 4:15 in a marathon. Keep following this schedule, choosing the higher mileages as you feel ready, and reassess your marathon target after the half-marathon in Week 9. Listen to your body, and ease off if you experience aches and pains.

WEEK	MONDAY	TUESDAY	WEDNESDAY
5	rest	1 M jog (see p. 95); 3–4 x 800 m, with 2-min recoveries (see p. 95); then 1 M jog	rest or 5 M slow (see p. 95)
6	rest	1 M jog; then 3 x 1200 m, with 4-min recoveries; then 1 M jog	rest or 5 M slow
7	rest	1 M jog; then 1200 m, 800 m, 400 m, 800 m, 1200 m, with recoveries half as long as the efforts; then 1 M jog	rest or 5 M slow
8	rest	1–2 M jog; then 8 x 400 m, with 2-min recoveries; then 1–2 M jog	rest or 5 M slow
9	rest	1 M jog; then 4–5 x 800 m, with 2-min recoveries; then 1 M jog	rest or 6 M slow
10	rest	1 M jog; then 4 x 1200 m, with 4-min recoveries; then 1 M jog	3–5 M slow
11	rest	1 M jog; then 400 m, 800 m, 400 m, 1600 m, 400 m, 800 m, 400 m, with recoveries half as long as the efforts; then 1 M jog	4–7 M slow
12	rest	1–2 M jog; then 10–12 x 400 m, with 2-min recoveries; then 1–2 M jog	rest or 5 M slow
13	rest	1 M jog; then 2400 m, 1200 m, 2400 m, with 4-min recoveries; 1 M jog	4–7 M slow
14	rest	1 M jog; then 4 x 800 m, with 2-min recoveries; then 1 M jog	5–6 M slow
15	rest	1–2 M jog; then 6–8 x 400 m, with 2-min recoveries; 1–2 M jog	rest or 6 M slow
16	rest	1 M jog, then 1–2 M steady, then 1 M jog	rest or 4–5 M slow

THURSDAY	FRIDAY	SATURDAY	SUNDAY
1 M slow, then 3–4 M steady (see p. 95), then 1 M slow	rest	5 M slow, off-road (see p. 95)	10–14 M slow
2 M slow, then 1–2 M brisk, then 2 M slow	rest	5 M slow, off-road	11–15 M slow
2 M slow, then 4 M steady, then 2 M slow	rest	4–5 M slow, off-road	10-mile to half-marathon race, or 12–16 M slow
4–5 M relaxed fartlek (see p. 95)	rest	4–5 M slow, off-road	11–15 M slow
1 M slow, then 3–5 M steady, then 1 M slow	rest	4–5 M slow, off-road	half-marathon race
1 M slow, then 4 M brisk, then 1 M slow	rest	4–5 M slow, off-road	14–18 M slow
5–6 M fartlek	rest	5 M slow, off-road	15–19 M slow
1 M slow, then 4–5 M steady	rest	4–5 M slow, off-road	13–15 M slow
2 M slow, then 1–3 M brisk, then 2 M slow	rest	4–5 M slow, off-road	18–20 M slow
6–7 M fartlek	rest	4–5 M slow, off-road	13–15 M slow or 10K to 10-mile race
2 M slow, then 1–2 M brisk, then 2 M slow	rest	4–5 M slow, off-road	8–10 M slow
4 M slow, inc. strides	rest	rest or 2–4 M slow	marathon

how's it going? ▶▶

how's it going? ▶▶

week 8— how's it going?

You are halfway toward your marathon goal—your body is becoming a more efficient running machine, as your muscle cells learn to process oxygen and use energy more effectively, and your cardiovascular system becomes stronger. Next week's half-marathon should give you a rough idea of your marathon potential:

2:15 = 5:00
2:00 = 4:26
1:48 = 3:58
1:35 = 3:28

week 12— how's it going?

Weeks 10, 11, and 13 are the most demanding in your schedule, but now you have three months of marathon training fitness under your belt. After Week 13, your preparation is almost complete—all you have to do is stay healthy, well-rested, and injury-free for two weeks. This is the time to get physiotherapy for any minor injuries, and fine-tune your strategy for eating and drinking before and during the run.

5 upper level

This level is for those who can run for 25–35 miles (40–56 km) over four to six days a week. It contains a fitness running schedule, a 10K and half-marathon schedule, and a marathon schedule. We have attached approximate time targets to the race schedules (40–50 minutes, 1:30–1:50 and 3:30–4:15 respectively), but it is more important that you select a schedule with an appropriate training volume for your current fitness.

level 5 fitness schedule

FOUR WEEKS REPEATABLE

Before you start you should be able to run for 40–45 minutes, five to six days per week, with regular speedwork.

To use the fitness schedule, first follow the main sessions. If you want to progress when you have comfortably completed the first four weeks, repeat the schedule, incorporating the variations in Cycle 2.

If you want to train longer, substitute your long Sunday runs for the shorter runs, which are designed more for people who do not normally do a long run. For non-marathon training, most coaches recommend a Sunday run of one-and-a-quarter to two hours.

WEEK	MONDAY	TUESDAY
1	rest or 25–40 mins slow	10 mins jog (see p. 95); then 8 x 2 mins (or 400 m) fast (see p. 95), with 90-sec jog recoveries; then 10 mins jog
CYCLE 2		add two repetitions
2	rest or 25–40 mins slow	10 mins slow, then 20–25 mins fartlek (see p. 95), then 10 mins slow
CYCLE 2		add 5 mins fartlek
3	rest or 25–40 mins slow	10 mins slow; then 1 min, 2 mins, 4 mins, 6 mins, 4 mins, 2 mins, 1 min (or 200 m, 400 m, 800 m, 1600 m, 800 m, 400 m, 200 m) fast, with half-length recoveries; then 10 mins slow
CYCLE 2		add 30 secs to each effort
4	rest or 25–40 mins slow	10 mins slow; then 4–5 x 4 mins (or 800 m), with 3-min jog recoveries, then 10 mins slow
CYCLE 2		add one repetition

how do I train for a 10-miler?

A half-marathon schedule is a good basis for 10-mile training. However, as well as decreasing the long runs by two or three miles, you can adapt the half-marathon schedules for a 10-mile race by running threshold sessions. For example, jog a 2-mile warm-up, then run 3–4 miles at 15–20 seconds per mile slower than your 10K speed, then jog a mile to cool down. Alternatively, as a long weekend or midweek run, run easy for 2 miles, then at 10-mile pace for 2 miles, then easy for 3 miles, then at 10-mile pace for 2 miles, then easy for a mile. This will get you used to both 10-mile pace and distance.

WEDNESDAY	THURSDAY	FRIDAY	SATURDAY	SUNDAY
30–40 mins slow (see p. 95)	30–40 mins slow, or: 10–15 mins jog; then 8–10 x 1-min steep hill climbs, jog down; then 10–15 mins jog	rest	30–40 mins slow	45–55 mins slow
	add 5–10 mins slow; or two hill repetitions			add 10 mins
30–40 mins slow	30–40 mins slow, or: 10 mins jog; then 2 x 10 mins brisk, with 5 mins jog recovery; then 10 mins jog	rest	30–40 mins slow	50–60 mins slow
	add 5–10 mins slow; or 2 mins each repetition			add 15 mins
35–50 mins slow	35–45 mins slow, or: 10–15 mins jog, then 20–25 mins long-burst fartlek	rest	35–45 mins slow, with strides (see p. 95)	55–65 mins slow
	add 5–10 mins slow; or 5mins fartlek			add 15 mins
35–50 mins slow	35–45 mins slow, or: 35–45 mins steady, on hilly route	rest	35–45 mins slow, with strides	race 5–10K, or run 60–70 mins slow
	add 5–10 mins			race 5–10 M, or add 15 mins

week 4— how's it going?

Be sure to take your time. If you are becoming frequently tired, or if you have persistent aches and pains, do not hesitate to replace a long or hard run with a shorter or easier one. If you have reached the end of Week 4 without problems, and you want to get ready for Level 6, progress to Cycle 2. Otherwise, repeat the first cycle until you feel comfortable with it. At the end of Cycle 2, either repeat the cycle or move up to Level 6.

5 10K & half-marathon schedules

Before you start you should be able to run 25–35 miles over five to six days a week.

HALF-MARATHON RUNNERS: The variations to your schedule are the figures in [brackets].

CROSS-TRAINING Supplementing your running with other activities (such as cycling, swimming, or rowing) is an excellent way of boosting your fitness with minimal injury risk. Strength and flexibility training—such as weights and yoga—also have great value.

WEEK	MONDAY	TUESDAY	WEDNESDAY
1	rest or 4–5 M slow	1.5 M jog (see p. 95); then 6 x 400 m, with 2-min recoveries; 1.5 M jog	4–5 M slow (see p. 95)
2	rest or 4–5 M slow	1.5 M jog; then 6 x 600 m, with 2.5-min recoveries; then 1.5 M jog; [3–4 x 1200 m with 3-min recoveries]	4–5 M slow
3	rest or 4–5 M slow	1.5 M jog; then 1 M measured time-trial; then 1.5 M jog	4–5 M slow [5–6 M]
4	rest or 4–5 M slow	2 M jog; then 2 x 200 m, 400 m, 800 m, 400 m, 200 m, with recoveries half as long, with extra 3 mins between sets; then 2 M jog	4–5 M slow [5–6 M]
5	rest or 4–5 M slow	1.5 M jog; then 6 x 800 m, with 3-min recoveries; then 1.5 M jog	5–6 M slow [7–8 M]
6	rest or 4–5 M slow	2 M jog; then 1 M measured time-trial; then 2 M jog [do Saturday's session]	5–6 M slow [7–8 M]
7	rest or 4–5 M slow	1.5 M jog; then 5 x 1200 m, with 3-min recoveries; then 1.5 M jog	5–6 M slow [8–9 M]
8	rest or 4–5 M slow	1.5 M jog; then 8 x 400 m, with 2-min recoveries; then 1.5 M jog [3–4 x 1 M, with 4-min recoveries]	4–5 M slow [8–9 M]
9	rest or 4–5 M slow	2 M jog; then 2 x 200 m, 400 m, 800 m, 400 m, 200 m (with recoveries half as long as the efforts), with an extra 3 mins between sets; 2 M jog	5–6 M slow
10	rest or 3–4 M slow	1 M jog, then 2 M brisk, then 2 M jog	5 M slow

HALF-MARATHON ONLY

approx. 40–50 minutes 10K; 1:30–1:50 half-marathon

THURSDAY	FRIDAY	SATURDAY	SUNDAY
5–6 M steady (see p. 95)	rest	10 mins slow, 15 mins brisk (see p. 95), 10 mins slow	6 M slow [7 M]
5–6 M steady	rest	10 mins slow, then 35 mins fartlek (see p. 95)	7 M slow [8 M]
5–6 M steady	rest	1.5 M jog; then 5 x 800 m, with 3-min recoveries; then 1.5 M jog	8 M slow [9 M]

how's it going? ▶▶

THURSDAY	FRIDAY	SATURDAY	SUNDAY
5–6 M steady	rest	10 mins slow, 25–30 mins brisk, 10 mins slow	6 M slow [7 M]
6–7 M steady	rest	10 mins slow, then 40 mins fartlek	8 M slow [9 M]
7–8 M steady	rest	2 M jog; then 12 x 1-min steep hill climbs, jogging down; then 2 M jog [4 M slow inc. strides]	9 M slow [10K race]

how's it going? ▶▶

THURSDAY	FRIDAY	SATURDAY	SUNDAY
7–8 M steady	rest	10 mins slow, 15 mins brisk, 10 mins slow	10 M slow [10–12 M]
4–5 M steady [7–8 M]	rest	35 mins slow, inc. strides [10 mins slow, then 35 mins fartlek]	10K race [12–13 M slow]
5–6 M steady	rest	10 mins slow, 15 mins brisk, 10 mins slow	7–9 M slow
5 M easy fartlek	rest	rest or 3 M easy, inc. optional strides	**half-marathon race**

how's it going?

week 4

You can give yourself a rough 10K time target on the basis of last Tuesday's one-mile time trial:

8 mins = 58 mins
7 mins = 51 mins
6 mins = 43 mins
5:30 = 39 mins
5 mins = 36 mins

week 6

For half-marathon runners, Sunday's 10K race should give you a good feeling for a half-marathon target:

58 mins = 2:15
51 mins = 1:57
47 mins = 1:48
43 mins = 1:39
39 mins = 1:30
38 mins = 1:26
36 mins = 1:21

marathon schedule (3:30–4:15)

Before you start you should be able to run 28–35 miles over five days a week, with regular long runs of 6–7 miles.

week 4—
how's it going?

Your aim so far is to grow comfortable with increasing mileage, so do not worry about how fast you are going. If you ran less than 42 minutes for 10K, however, you have the potential to beat 3:30 in your marathon. Keep following this schedule for now, choosing the higher mileages as you feel ready, and reassess your marathon target after the half-marathon in Week 9. Remember that if you experience persistent aches and pains, take some rest. If your pain does not respond to rest, seek professional advice.

WEEK	MONDAY	TUESDAY	WEDNESDAY
1	rest	1.5 M jog; 4–5 x 800 m, with 2-min recoveries (see p. 95); 1–1.5 M jog	4–6 M slow (see p. 95)
2	rest	1.5 M jog; then 2–3 x 1600 m, with 3-min recoveries; then 1–1.5 M jog	4–6 M slow
3	rest	1–1.5 M jog; then 400 m, 800 m, 1200 m; 1200 m (optional); 800 m, 400 m, with recoveries half as long as the efforts; then 1–1.5 M jog	4–6 M slow
4	rest	1–2 M jog; then 8–10 x 400 m, with 90-sec recoveries; then 1–2 M jog	4–6 M slow
5	rest or 3 M slow	1–1.5 M jog; then 5–6 x 800 m, with 2-min recoveries; 1–1.5 M jog	4–5 M slow
6	rest or 4 M slow	1–1.5 M jog; then 3–4 x 1600 m, with 3-min recoveries; then 1–1.5 M jog	4–5 M slow
7	rest or 4 M slow	6 M fartlek, or if not racing on Sunday, do 1–1.5 M jog; then 1600 m, 1200 m, 800 m, 1200 m, 1600 m, with recoveries half as long as the efforts; then 1–1.5 M jog	5–7 M slow
8	rest or 4 M slow	1–2 M jog; then 8–10 x 400 m, with 90-sec recoveries; then 1–2 M jog; go easy if you raced hard on Sunday	4–5 M slow

why do I need speedwork for a marathon?

The benefits of speedwork go far beyond teaching your body to run at a sprint. Running fast, especially repeatedly, enables you to use oxygen more effectively, and raises the threshold at which your muscles start to tire. It also strengthens your legs, and burns far more calories than normal running, even hours after the session. These things all pay dividends for a marathon runner. Mentally, speedwork is important, too. The ability to run on tired legs is invaluable in a marathon, and speedwork is a concentrated way of achieving this.

THURSDAY	FRIDAY	SATURDAY	SUNDAY
5–6 M starting slow, finishing faster	rest	5 M slow, off-road	7–10 M slow
1 M slow; 3–4 M steady (see p. 95); 1 M slow	rest	5 M slow, off-road	9–12 M slow
2 M slow, then 2–3 M brisk, then 2 M slow	rest	5–6 M slow, off-road	11–14 M slow
5–7 M relaxed fartlek (see p. 95)	rest	4–6 M slow, off-road	10K race (aim for 42–51 minutes)
1 M slow, then 4 M steady, then 1 M slow	rest	5 M slow, off-road	13–16 M slow
2 M slow, then 1–2 M brisk, then 2 M slow	rest	5 M slow, off-road	15–18 M slow
5 M steady	rest	5–7 M slow, off-road	10 M to half-marathon race, or 14–16 M slow
4–5 M relaxed fartlek	rest	4–5 M slow, off-road	14–16 M slow

◂◂ how's it going?

week 8— how's it going?

You are halfway toward your marathon goal already. Your body is becoming a more efficient running machine. Do not worry if it does not feel that way. In the last two months you have increased your weekly mileage by 50 percent and doubled the length of your long runs, all of which is requiring extra fitness. However, if the easier weeks (weeks 4, 8, and 12) leave you feeling drained, it is time to ease off. Just run easy and short for up to a week, then try easing back into the schedule.

how's it going? ▸▸

marathon schedule (3:30–4:15)

Although by this stage you might find the training tough, remember that it is worth it for the sake of doing the right preparation to reach your goal of completing a marathon in under 4:15. And there is nothing like that feeling of achievement when you cross the finishing line.

week 12—how's it going?

Weeks 10, 11, and 13 are the most demanding in your schedule, so do not be surprised if you feel tired. The good news is that after week 13 you ease down dramatically, safe in the knowledge that you have three months of marathon training fitness behind you. Your preparation is almost complete—all you have to do now is stay healthy, well rested, and injury-free for two weeks. Now is the time to get physiotherapy for any minor injuries, and fine-tune your strategy for eating and drinking before and during your run, if you have not done so already (see pages 30–31 for more about this).

running targets

The half-marathon in Week 9 should give you a rough idea of your marathon potential:

2:00 = 4:26
1:48 = 3:58
1:35 = 3:28
1:29 = 3:14

Your best half-marathon plan, if you are unsure of your potential, is to start conservatively and speed up very gradually every 3 miles (5 km).

WEEK	MONDAY	TUESDAY
9	rest or 4 M slow	6 M fartlek
10	rest or 4 M slow	1–1.5 M jog; then 3–5 x 1600 m, with 3-min recoveries; then 1–1.5 M jog; go easy if you raced hard on Sunday
11	rest or 4 M slow	1–1.5 M jog; then 400 m (optional), 800 m, 400 m, 1200 m, 400 m, 1600 m, 400 m, 1200 m, 400 m, 800 m, 400 m (optional), with recoveries half as long as the efforts; then 1–1.5 M jog
12	rest or 4 M slow	1–2 M jog; then 12–14 x 400 m, with 90-sec recoveries; then 1–2 M jog
13	rest or 4 M slow	1.5 M jog; then 3200 m, 1600 m, 3200 m, with 4-min recoveries; then 1.5 M jog
14	rest	1–1.5 M jog; then 4–5 x 800 m, with 2-min recoveries; then 1–1.5 M jog
15	rest or 4 M slow	1–2 M jog; then 8–10 x 400 m, with 90-sec recoveries; then 1–2 M jog; go easy if you raced hard on Sunday
16	rest or 4–5 M slow	1 M jog, then 1–2 M steady, then 1 M jog

sustained an injury?

If injury prevents you from running properly in the final month of the schedules, you should seriously consider deferring your marathon. If you have been forced to miss more than two weeks of training since you started the schedules, it may be wise to revise your original time target (at least run the first half of the marathon slower than you would have planned). For more race-day advice, see pages 90–91.

WEDNESDAY	THURSDAY	FRIDAY	SATURDAY	SUNDAY
5–8 M slow	1 M slow, then 5 M steady	rest	5 M slow, off-road	half-marathon race (aim for 1:35–1:58)
4–6 M slow	1 M slow, then 4 M brisk, then 1 M slow	rest	4–5 M slow, off-road	17–20 M slow
4–7 M slow	5–6 M fartlek	rest	5 M slow, off-road	19–22 M slow
4–5 M slow	5–6 M steady	rest	4–5 M slow, off-road	15–18 M slow
5–9 M slow	2 M slow, then 2–3 M brisk, then 2 M slow	rest	5–6 M slow, off-road	18–20 M slow
6–7 M slow	7–8 M fartlek	rest	4–5 M slow, off-road	13–15 M slow or 10K to half-marathon race
4–6 M slow	2 M slow, then 2–3 M brisk, then 2 M slow	rest	5 M slow, off-road	8–10 M slow
4–5 M slow	4 M slow, inc. strides	rest	rest or 2–4 M slow	**marathon**

upper level

This level is for those who have built up to running 30–40 miles (48–65 km) over six or seven days a week. It contains a fitness running schedule, a 10K and half-marathon schedule, and a marathon schedule. We have attached approximate time targets to the race schedules (34–40 minutes, 1:15–1:30 and 2:50–3:30 respectively), but it is more important

level 6 fitness schedules

Before you start you should be able to run for 40–50 minutes, six to seven days a week, including regular speedwork.

To use this fitness schedule, first follow the main sessions. If you want to progress when you have comfortably completed the first four-week cycle, repeat the schedule, incorporating the variations in Cycle 2.

Because you may already enjoy runs of 90 minutes or more on Sundays, you should feel free to substitute them for the shorter Sunday runs, which are designed for people who do not normally do a long run. For nonmarathon training, most coaches recommend a Sunday run of one-and-a-quarter to two hours.

WEEK	MONDAY	TUESDAY
1	30–40 mins slow	10 mins jog (see p. 95); then 12 x 2 mins (or 400 m) fast (see p. 95), with 90-sec jog recoveries; then 10 mins jog
CYCLE **2**		add two repetitions
2	30–40 mins slow	10 mins slow, then 20–25 mins hard fartlek (see p. 95), then 10 mins slow
CYCLE **2**		add 5 mins fartlek
3	30–50 mins slow	10 mins slow; then 6 mins, 4 mins, 2 mins, 1 min, 2 mins, 4 mins, 6 mins (or 1600 m, 800 m, 400 m, 200 m, 400 m, 800 m, 1600 m) fast, with half-length recoveries; then 10 mins slow
CYCLE **2**		add 30 secs to each effort
4	30–50 mins slow	10 mins slow; then 5–6 x 4 mins (or 800 m) fast, with 3-min jog recoveries, then 10 mins slow
CYCLE **2**		add one repetition

that you select a schedule with the right training volume for your fitness. Do not be afraid to drop back a few weeks if training is causing you pain. It is a far greater achievement to run well on a low training volume than to achieve an average run on a high one.

speedwork guide

Your speedwork pace should simply be one that you can maintain strongly but evenly, and it will vary according to the length of your repetitions and recoveries. Here is a guide to what you can expect to be capable of averaging:

40 mins for 10K: 400 m = 1:25; 800 m = 3:00; 1200 m = 4:50
38 mins for 10K: 400 m = 1:22; 800 m = 2:53; 1200 m = 4:40
35 mins for 10K: 400 m = 1:15; 800 m = 2:40; 1200 m = 4:15

WEDNESDAY	THURSDAY	FRIDAY	SATURDAY	SUNDAY
35–45 mins slow (see p. 95)	35–45 mins slow, or: 10- to 15-mins jog; then 10–12 x 1-min steep hill climbs, jogging back down; then 10- to 15-mins jog	rest	35–45 mins slow	50–60 mins slow
	add 5–10 mins slow; or two hill repetitions			add 10 mins
35–45 mins slow	35–45 mins slow, or: 10-mins jog, then 2 x 10 mins brisk, with 5-min jog recovery; then 10-mins jog	rest	35–45 mins slow	55–65 mins slow
	add 5–10 mins slow; or 2 mins to each repetition			add 15 mins
40–55 mins slow	40–55 mins slow, or: 10- to 15-mins jog, then 25–30 mins long-burst fartlek	rest	40–50 mins slow, with strides (see p. 95)	60–70 mins slow
	add 5–10 mins slow; or 5 mins fartlek			add 15 mins
40–55 mins slow	40–50 mins slow, or: 40–50 mins steady, on hilly route	rest	40–50 mins slow, with strides	race 5K, or run 65–75 mins slow
	add 5–10 mins			race 5K to half-marathon, or add 15 mins

week 4— how's it going?

Be sure to take your time. If you have persistent aches and pains, do not hesitate to replace a long or hard run with a shorter or easier one. If you have reached the end of Week 4 with no problems, and you want to increase your fitness, progress to Cycle 2. Otherwise, repeat the first cycle for as long as you wish.

10K & half-marathon schedules

(APPROX 34- TO 40-MIN 10K; 1:15–1:30 HALF-MARATHON)

week 3—how's it going?

10K runners: You can give yourself a rough 10K time target on the basis of Tuesday's one-mile time trial:

6:30 = 47 mins
6 mins = 43 mins
5:30 = 39 mins
5 mins = 36 mins
4:40 = 34 mins

Half-marathoners: It is harder to predict half-marathon times from a mile run, but they potentially equate to 1:48, 1:39, 1:30, 1:21, and 1:15 respectively.

If you ran the mile in more than 6:30 that is fine, as long as you are comfortable with the mileage and intensity of this schedule.

week 6—how's it going?

10K runners: Don't worry if last week's time trial was not faster than the first one—you have just had three weeks of training. Still use you latest mile time as a guide (see above). Set off on race day at your target pace, then speed up in the last 2 miles (3 km) if you feel strong.

Half-marathoners: You can gauge a half-marathon time from Sunday's 10K race:

47 mins = 1:48
43 mins = 1:39
39 mins = 1:30
38 mins = 1:26
36 mins = 1:21

WEEK	MONDAY	TUESDAY
1	rest or 5–6 M slow	1.5 M jog (see p. 95); 8 x 400 m, with 2-min recoveries; 1.5 M jog
2	rest or 5–6 M slow	1.5 M jog; 8 x 600 m, with 2.5-min recoveries; 1.5 M jog [4–5 x 1200 m with 3-min recoveries]
3	rest or 5–6 M slow	2 M jog; then 1 M measured time-trial; then 2 M jog
4	rest or 5–6 M slow	2 M jog; 2 x 200 m, 400 m, 600 m, 800 m, 600 m, 400 m, 200 m, recoveries half as long as efforts, extra 3 mins between sets; 2 M jog
5	rest or 5–6 M slow	1.5 M jog; then 8 x 800 m, with 3-min recoveries; then 1.5 M jog
6	rest or 5–6 M slow	2 M jog; then 1 M measured time-trial; then 2 M jog [do Saturday's session]
7	rest or 5–6 M slow	1.5 M jog; then 6 x 1200 m, with 3-min recoveries; then 1.5 M jog
8	rest or 5–6 M slow	1.5 M jog; then 9 x 400 m, with 2-min recoveries; then 1.5 M jog [4–5 x 1 M, with 4-min recoveries]
9	rest or 5–6 M slow	2 M jog; 2 x 200 m, 400 m, 600 m, 800 m, 600 m, 400 m, 200 m, recoveries half as long as efforts, 3 mins between sets; 2 M jog
10	rest or 3–4 M slow	1 M jog, then 2 M brisk, then 2 M jog

half-marathon only

Before you start you should be able to run 30–40 miles (50–65 km) every week.

Half-marathon runners—the variations to your schedule are the figures in [brackets].

WEDNESDAY	THURSDAY	FRIDAY	SATURDAY	SUNDAY
5–6 M slow (see p. 95)	6–7 M steady (see p. 95)	rest	10 mins slow, 20 mins brisk, 10 mins slow	8 M slow [9 M]
5–6 M slow	6–7 M steady	rest	10 mins slow, then 35 mins fartlek (see p. 95)	9 M slow [10 M]
5–6 M slow [6–7 M]	6–7 M steady	rest	1.5 M jog; then 6 x 800 m, with 3-min recoveries; then 1.5 M jog	10 M slow [11 M]

◀◀ how's it going?

WEDNESDAY	THURSDAY	FRIDAY	SATURDAY	SUNDAY
5–6 M slow [6–7 M]	6–7 M steady	rest	10 mins slow, 25–30 mins brisk, 10 mins slow	8 M slow [6 M]
6–7 M slow [8–9 M]	7–8 M steady	rest	10 mins slow, then 40 mins fartlek	10 M slow [11 M]
6–7 M slow [8–9 M]	8–9 M steady	rest	2 M jog; 12 x 1-min steep hill climbs, jog down; 2 M jog [4–5 M slow, inc. strides]	11 M slow [10K race]

◀◀ how's it going?

WEDNESDAY	THURSDAY	FRIDAY	SATURDAY	SUNDAY
6–7 M slow [9–10 M]	7–8 M steady	rest	10 mins slow, 20 mins brisk, 10 mins slow	12 M slow [12–14 M]
4–5 M slow [9–10 M]	6–7 M steady [7–8 M]	rest	35 mins slow, inc. strides [10 mins slow, then 40 mins fartlek]	10K race [14–15 M slow]
6–7 M slow	6–7 M steady	rest	10 mins slow, 20 mins brisk, 10 mins slow	8–10 M slow
6 M slow	5–7 M easy fartlek	rest	4 M easy, inc. strides	half-marathon race

6

marathon schedule (2:50–3:30)

Before you begin this schedule you should be able to run 30–40 miles (48–65 km) over six or seven days a week.

WEEK	MONDAY	TUESDAY	WEDNESDAY
1	4 M slow	1–2 M jog (see p. 95); then 5–6 x 800 m, with 2-min recoveries; then 1–2 M jog	5–6 M slow (see p. 95)
2	4 M slow	1–2 M jog; 3–4 x 1600 m, with 3-min recoveries; then 1–2 M jog	5–6 M slow
3	4 M slow	1–2 M jog; then 400 m, 800 m, 1200 m, 1600 m (optional), 1200 m, 800 m, 400 m, with recoveries half as long as the efforts; then 1–2 M jog	5–6 M slow
4	5 M slow	1–2 M jog; then 10–12 x 400 m, with 90-sec recoveries; then 1–2 M jog	5–7 M slow
5	4 M slow	1–2 M jog; then 6–7 x 800 m, with 2-min recoveries; then 1–2 M jog	5–6 M slow
6	4 M slow	1–2 M jog; then 4–5 x 1600 m, with 3-min recoveries; then 1–2 M jog	4–5 M slow
7	4 M slow	6 M fartlek, or if not racing Sunday, do 1–2 M jog; 1600 m, 1200 m, 800 m, optional 400 m and 800 m, 1200 m, 1600 m, with recoveries half as long as the efforts; 1–2 M jog	6–7 M slow
8	4 M slow	1–2 M jog; 10–12 x 400 m, with 90-sec recoveries; 1–2 M jog; go easy if you raced hard on Sunday	4–5 M slow

week 4— how's it going?

Your aim so far is to grow comfortable with increasing mileage, so don't worry about how fast you are going. Use the following as a guide to potential marathon times:

42 mins = 3:30
40 mins = sub-3:15
36 mins = 3:00
35 mins = 2:50

Whatever your pace, listen to your body, and ease off if you experience persistent aches or pains. If your pain does not respond to rest, seek professional advice.

THURSDAY	FRIDAY	SATURDAY	SUNDAY
1–2 M jog; 10–14 x 1-min steep hill climbs, jogging back down; then 1–2 M jog	5 M slow or rest	5 M slow, off-road	8–11 M slow
1 M jog; then 20–30 mins fartlek (see p. 95); 1 M jog	5 M slow or rest	5 M slow, off-road	10–13 M slow
1.5 M jog; then 2 x 10 mins brisk (see p. 95), with 5-mins jog recovery; then 1.5 M jog	5 M slow or rest	5 M slow, off-road	12–15 M slow
1 M jog; then 20–30 mins fartlek (longer efforts); then 1 M jog	5 M slow or rest	5 M slow, off-road, inc. optional 2–3 M steady	10K race (aim for 35–42 minutes)
1–2 M jog; then 12–16 x 1-min hill climbs, jogging back down; 1–2 M jog	5 M slow or rest	5 M slow, off-road	14–17 M slow
1 M jog; then 25–35 mins fartlek (shorter efforts); then 1 M jog	4 M slow or rest	5 M slow, off-road	16–20 M slow, inc. 5–7 M steady
1.5 M jog; then 2 x 15 mins brisk, with 5-min jog recovery; then 1.5 M jog	5 M slow or rest	5 M slow, off-road, inc. optional 2–3 M steady	10 M to half-marathon race, or 14–16 M slow
1–2 M jog; then 4–7 x 2- to 3-mins hill climbs, jog back down; 1 M jog	rest	4 M slow, off-road	16–18 M slow

week 8— how's it going?

You are halfway toward your marathon goal already. Your body is becoming a more efficient running machine. In the last two months you have increased your weekly mileage by 50 percent and doubled the length of your long run, all of which is requiring your extra fitness. Next week's half-marathon should give you a rough idea of your marathon potential:

1:40 = 3:40
1:35 = 3:28
1:29 = 3:14
1:22 = 2:58
1:20 = 2:52

how's it going? ▸▸

weeks 9–16   ▸▸

marathon schedule (2:50–3:30)

WEEK	MONDAY	TUESDAY	WEDNESDAY
9	5 M slow	6 M fartlek	7–8 M slow
10	5 M slow	1–2 M jog; then 4–6 x 1600 m, with 3-min recoveries; then 1–2 M jog	5–8 M slow
11	5 M slow	1–2 M jog; then 400 m, 800 m, 400 m, 1200 m, 400 m, 1600 m, 400 m, 1200 m, 400 m, 800 m, 400 m, with half-length recoveries; then 1–2 M jog	7 M slow
12	4 M slow	1–2 M jog; then 14–18 x 400 m, with 90-sec recoveries; then 1–2 M jog	4–5 M slow
13	5 M slow	1–2 M jog; then 4800 m, 3200 m, 1600 m, with 4-min recoveries; then 1–2 M jog	10 M slow
14	5 M slow	1–2 M jog; then 5–7 x 800 m, with 2-min recoveries; then 1–2 M jog	6–7 M slow
15	5 M slow	1–2 M jog; then 10–12 x 400 m, with 90-sec recoveries; then 1–2 M jog; go easy if you raced hard on Sunday	6 M slow
16	rest or 4–5 M slow	1 M jog, then 1–2 M steady, then 1 M jog	5 M slow

training twice a day

Adding a few easy morning runs of three or four miles to a normal routine is a simple way of boosting weekly mileage without requiring extremely long sessions. Kenyan runners do this every day without even regarding it as mileage. But do you need it? Certainly not if you run more than 50 miles a week, or are training for a marathon of more than three hours. It could be useful if you want to run seven days of mileage in six days.

THURSDAY	FRIDAY	SATURDAY	SUNDAY
1 M jog; then 30–40 mins fartlek (longer efforts); then 1 M jog	5 M slow or rest	5 M slow, off-road, inc. 2–3 M steady	half-marathon race (aim for 1:17–1:35)
1–2 M jog; then 2 (7 x 1-min) hill climbs, with 3 mins between sets; 1–2 M	5 M slow or rest	6 M slow, off-road	18–20 M slow, inc. 5–8 M steady
1.5 M jog; then 3 x 10–12 mins brisk, with 4-min jog recoveries; then 1.5 M jog	5 M slow or rest	5 M slow, off-road	19–22 M slow
1 M jog; then 20–30 mins fartlek (shorter efforts); then 1 M jog	5 M slow or rest	5 M slow, off-road	17–18 M slow, inc. 6–8 M steady
1–2 M jog; then 6–10 x 2- to 3-min hill climbs, jogging down; 1–2 M jog	5 M slow or rest	5 M slow, off-road	20–22 M slow
1 M jog; then 20–30 mins fartlek; then 1 M jog	5 M slow or rest	5 M slow, off-road, inc. 2–3 M steady	13–15 M slow or 10K to half-marathon race
1.5 M jog; then 2 x 10 mins brisk, with 4-min jog recovery; then 1.5 M jog	5 M slow or rest	5 M slow, off-road	9–11 M slow
5 M slow, inc. strides	rest or 4 M slow	rest or 4 M slow	marathon

week 12—how's it going?

Weeks 10, 11, and 13 are the most demanding in your schedule, so do not be surprised if you feel tired. After Week 13 you ease down, knowing that you have achieved three months of marathon training fitness. Your preparation is almost complete—all you have to do now is stay healthy, well rested, and injury-free for two weeks. Now is the time to get physiotherapy for any minor injuries, and fine-tune your strategy for eating and drinking before and during your run, if you have not done so already (see pages 30–31 for more about this).

3

how to...

...run a marathon

...lose weight and keep it off

...enjoy running for the rest of your life

...run a marathon

Running a marathon can be one of the most fulfilling experiences of your life. You will cross the finish line feeling exhausted, exhilarated, close to tears and vowing you will never do it again—until next time. In many ways it is a condensed version of your whole running life—and that includes only

getting out of it what you put in. If you do want to rise to the challenge of the marathon—and if you want to enjoy it, we don't recommend that you attempt a marathon until you've been running for at least a year—you can find whole books written on the subject. Here is the in-a-nutshell version.

the training

follow a schedule

It is essential to run regularly and progressively. (Don't believe the friend of a friend who says he got around comfortably after only one five-mile run a week for a month.) A good schedule will sensibly build your endurance and speed, until at the end of 16 weeks (or thereabout) you're ready to give the marathon your best shot. It will combine long runs, fast runs, and rest to keep you motivated, injury-free (hopefully), and strong.

run fast

One or two speed sessions each week will strengthen your legs and teach them to run better when they are tired.

run long

There are no shortcuts around essential endurance-building preparation. Aim for five to eight runs of between 16 and 22 miles, spaced evenly over the final 12 weeks of your marathon training.

rest

This is essential. Do not run consecutive hard days, and do take one or two days off a week, and an easy week each month.

race week

1 Do nothing more than easy runs with a few short sets of strides this week. Your aim is to stay in shape but well rested.

2 Do not worry about carbo-loading: continue to eat normal portions and your muscles' fuel reserves will automatically fill as your mileage decreases.
(See pages 30–31 for more about eating for a marathon.)

3 In the last two days, keep especially well hydrated and stay off your feet as much as possible.

4 Do not be tempted by new clothes, shoes, gadgets, or energy foods for race day. You should have tried and tested everything on several long training runs.

5 Plan your travel, and prepare a racing clothes list as well as dry, warm post-race clothes for the baggage bus. Put aside some warm, disposable layers for the start.

6 Prepare a rough pace plan to write on your hand or race number for race day.

7 If you are ill or you have been injured, seriously consider postponing your marathon—26.2 miles is incredibly unforgiving, even for a healthy body.

race day

1 Allow yourself plenty of time to eat and digest a simple, tried-and-tested breakfast of about 400 calories.

2 Consider taking strictly timed one-minute walk breaks every mile. This technique can work even for four-hour marathon runners, and will leave you feeling as fresh as if you had only run a half-marathon.

3 Don't waste valuable energy weaving through the crowds in the first couple of miles. Treat it as a natural warm-up.

4 Hold yourself back, especially in the early miles. Only if you get to mile 20 feeling great should you consider speeding up.

5 Drink at every opportunity, even if it means an occasional toilet stop. Dehydration is one of the main factors in "hitting the wall."

6 Aim to replace up to 600 calories of energy on the run, with gels, easy-to-digest candy, or sports drinks. Make sure you've tested them in training.

7 Cross that finish line with an unbelievable sense of pride—completing a marathon is an amazing achievement.

...lose weight and keep it off

Sadly, there are no secrets to weight loss: you simply have to burn more calories than you eat. The hard news is that there are no shortcuts, no matter what the dieting industry tries to tell you. The good news is that combining regular, sensible exercise with a reasonably healthy diet will give you better long-term results than any other method. And losing weight by an exercise-based plan won't just make you look good, either. Your whole body will be healthier and more efficient, and you will be boosted by the confidence that comes with achieving something regularly. The best results come with moderation and a positive attitude.

how to eat to lose weight

■ You could construct a detailed eating plan based on a calculation of your daily calorie needs, but as a first step it is best to take an honest look at what you eat in a typical day, and resolve to improve one aspect every two weeks. (See pages 24–25 for more information about food types.)

■ Try substituting snacks such as chocolate and chips with fruit, nuts, carrot sticks, or bagels. Take them into work and keep them by your desk. Similarly, substitute one or two red-meat-based meals a week with vegetarian options (see pages 26–27 for advice on a balanced diet).

■ Eat little and often through the day, and try not to eat to the point of discomfort at mealtimes. Your body processes food far more effectively in small amounts.

■ Avoid fad diets. No matter how they are presented, many diets achieve fast results simply by slashing calorie intake to an unhealthy level. This is why you can often end up putting the weight back on again when your body demands a return to what it sees as a normal calorie intake. For healthy, sustainable weight loss, aim for a daily deficit of no more than 1000 calories—preferably closer to 500.

the five essentials of weight loss

1 Do everything in moderation. That means not using crash diets, and not trying to run five miles on your first run.

2 Build up your running slowly but regularly—a routine is essential.

3 Aim for specific, attainable goals—both for your running and your weight loss—and reward yourself for achieving them.

4 Make changes to your diet one by one, and don't deny yourself everything you enjoy.

5 Be patient. Exercise and eat better and you will lose weight, even if it takes time.

how to exercise to lose weight

■ Start by alternating small amounts of walking and jogging—even as little as two minutes' walking and one minute's jogging, repeated for 30 minutes. You will end up doing far more exercise in each session than if you tried to jog nonstop, and time spent exercising is what burns calories and sheds weight.

■ Consider a couple of weeks of regular brisk walking before you start to run, and if you are more than 20 percent above your ideal weight, take up regular nonweight-bearing exercise such as cycling or swimming first.

■ Be committed. Ideally, follow a schedule (such as the ones described in this book) that will provide variety and progression. At least tell yourself that you will run for 20–30 minutes at a time, three or four times a week. Anything more will be a bonus.

■ Get into a routine. Planning your runs for the same times and days each week makes it far easier to do them. All runners find that a run left to chance almost inevitably does not happen.

■ Enjoy your running! Relish the time to yourself, or the opportunity to run in peaceful places. And if you can run with a friend, value the time together. If running does not let you enjoy the pace, slow down!

...enjoy running for the rest of your life

It is a privilege to be able to run , so be thankful for it—and be proud of every small step you make towards this goal. Here's how to stay healthy, motivated, and fulfilled for a lifetime of satisfying and effective running.

pace yourself

Run at your own pace, whatever that may be. Always run to suit your level of fitness.

socialize

Run with friends—this is absolutely the best running tip there is. You will motivate each other and enjoy time together in the bargain.

be inspired

Remember what it is you like about running, and cherish that feeling. Keep a record of whether each run makes you feel better or worse than before you went out. The results will speak for themselves.

help out

Give something back—help to marshal some races, learn to be a coach, or be more active in your local running club. You will feel more valuable, and have a positive impact on other runners.

set goals

Set yourself new targets. Try tackling a distance or discipline you have never tried before—such as an ultra (a race beyond marathon distance), or a two-day navigation race.

enjoy variety

Try not to do the same run more than twice a week. Ideally, mix speedwork, long runs, and super-relaxed recovery runs, and choose a range of on- and off-road routes if you can.

race

Enter races—these are substantial and confidence boosting markers of your progress.

be yourself

Finally, only be the runner that you want to be. It is a privilege to be able to run. Do not let anyone tell you that you have to enjoy that privilege in a certain way.

glossary

BRISK—Faster than conversational pace, but not so fast as to leave you panting. Around 85 percent of your working heart rate, or half-marathon race pace.

CARBOHYDRATE, COMPLEX—Foods made from long-chain molecules. They often release slow, sustained energy (see glycemic index).

CARBOHYDRATE, SIMPLE—Foods made from single molecules. They often release energy in short peaks (see glycemic index).

FARTLEK—"Speed play": random-length fast and slow bursts during a normal run.

FAST—A pace at which you finish a training run feeling you couldn't have given any more. Around 85–90 percent of your working heart rate, or 5K–10K race pace.

GAIT—The movement of the body during running. Most specifically, the movement of the foot and ankle, from landing on the heel to pushing off from the toes.

GLYCEMIC INDEX—A ranking of how quickly foods release their energy into the body.

OFF-ROAD—Trails, forest tracks, grassland... anything that is not concrete or asphalt. At its most extreme, it means taking the straightest line possible across country.

OVERPRONATION—Excessive inward rolling of the foot and ankle during the gait cycle. It's common, but if uncorrected it can lead to strain-related injuries.

PRONATION—the natural inward rolling of the foot and ankle during running and walking. It occurs just after the heel lands on the ground, and is essential to absorb shock. (See also overpronation and underpronation.)

RECOVERIES—The rest intervals in between fast efforts in speedwork. Ideally, a slow jog that allows your heart rate to drop to 120–130.

RECOVERY RUNS—Easy runs designed to keep the body supple, flush out toxins, and burn calories. Usually scheduled for the days after hard runs or races.

REPETITION—One of the periods of fast running during a speed session.

RESTING HEART RATE—Your lowest normal heart rate; best taken just after you wake up.

SLOW—A pace at which you could comfortably hold a conversation. The best speed for recovery runs; below 65 percent of your working heart rate.

SPEEDWORK—Structured, fast-paced training sessions designed to raise fitness, running speed, and running economy. Usually composed of fast efforts alternated with slow recoveries.

STEADY—The pace at which you might complete a long training run. Only just conversational; around 75 percent of your working heart rate, or marathon race pace.

STRIDES—Sets of brisk, loping 100 m runs to limber up the legs and raise the heart rate before a race or speed session. Usually done after a warm-up jog and light stretching.

UNDERPRONATION—Inadequate inward rolling of the foot and ankle during the gait cycle. If uncorrected with shoes that encourage foot motion it can lead to impact-related injuries.

WORKING HEART RATE (WHR)—The full range of your heart rate, between your resting pulse and your maximum.

index

acknowledgments

Warm thanks to my friends and colleagues Steven Seaton, Steve Smythe, Nick Troop, Bud Baldaro, Peta Bee, Eleanor Grey, Alison Fletcher and Nicola Wright for their insightful comments during the writing of this book.

Special thanks to Asics, New Balance, and Saucony, for providing running shoes; many thanks also to Sweatshop for kindly providing clothing and equipment.

Additional photography: Mike Good (pages 32–35).

Every effort has been made to credit everybody that appears in this book, and we apologize in advance for any unintentional omissions. We would be pleased to insert the appropriate acknowledgment in any subsequent edition of this publication.